Rob Goss first came to Japan in 1999 to teach English for a year. Two years at the most was the plan. Like so many other former English teachers, however, Rob has ended up staying far longer in Tokyo without really knowing why. Cupid's arrow certainly played a part, as did the pitter-patter of part-Japanese, part-British baby feet that followed. Living in a metropolis that never ceases to amaze has helped too. Then there's having a job he loves—writing about Japan for magazines such as *Time* and *National Geographic Traveler* and, at latest count, some 70 other magazines, book publishers and newspapers around the globe.

© Ben Simmons

Judith Clancy served in the Peace Corps in Korea from 1967 to 1969, bringing her to this part of the world. Fulfilling a childhood dream, she came to live in Kyoto in 1970. The culture captivated her from the start and became an affair of the heart as she learned the language, Ikebana and the tea ceremony. During that time, she taught at several universities and worked in a major Japanese company. She is the author of *Exploring Kyoto: On Foot in the Ancient Capital*; *Kyoto: City of Zen*; *Kyoto Machiya Restaurant Guide*; *Kyoto Gardens*; and *The Alluring World of Geiko and Maiko*.

Published by Tuttle Publishing, an imprint of Periplus Editions (HK) Ltd

www.tuttlepublishing.com

Copyright © 2018 Periplus Editions (HK) Ltd

ISBN: 978-4-8053-1474-6
(*Previously published under ISBN 978-4-8053-1178-3*)

Distributed by

North America, Latin America & Europe
Tuttle Publishing
364 Innovation Drive
North Clarendon, VT 05759-9436 U.S.A.
Tel: 1 (802) 773-8930
Fax: 1 (802) 773-6993
info@tuttlepublishing.com
www.tuttlepublishing.com

Japan
Tuttle Publishing
Yaekari Building, 3rd Floor
5-4-12 Osaki
Shinagawa-ku
Tokyo 141-0032
Tel: (81) 3 5437-0171
Fax: (81) 3 5437-0755
sales@tuttle.co.jp
www.tuttle.co.jp

Asia Pacific
Berkeley Books Pte. Ltd.
3 Kallang Sector #04-01,
Singapore 349278
Tel: (65) 67412178
Fax: (65) 67412179
inquiries@periplus.com.sg
www.tuttlepublishing.com

21 20 19   10 9 8 7 6 5 4 3 2

Printed in China   1910CM

TUTTLE TRAVEL PACK

JAPAN
Revised Edition

Rob Goss & Judith Clancy

TUTTLE Publishing

Tokyo | Rutland, Vermont | Singapore

Unforgettable Japan

Japan seen from afar and Japan experienced in the flesh are poles apart. I grew up in a sleepy English village, and before I first came to Japan more than a decade ago all I knew of the country were images of geisha and sumo, packed commuter trains, cool video arcades and city streets drenched in neon—the things that occupy the narrow gaze of many a travel magazine and documentary.

Japan, of course, does have all the above. Many of them make up my earliest memories of living in Tokyo. The first time I had to take a morning rush-hour train, I remember feeling as if I were binding on for a 300-person scrum, elbows flying and the tops of other commuters' heads occasionally cracking me under the jaw, a downside to having become relatively tall overnight. A few days later, my first experience of Shinjuku was like being thrown into a Philip K. Dick novel: flashing lights, buildings blocking out the sky, sirens, shoulder bumps from the crowds and blasts of noise and air-conditioning from every shop front I passed. It was fantastic.

But it didn't take long to discover that the stereotyped guidebook images were anything but typical of Japan. The Japanese don't spend half their time bowing deeply and munching on sushi. Girls very rarely aspire to be geisha, nor boys sumo wrestlers. Walk into any good *izakaya* (pub-cum-restaurant) and the staid, reserved image often painted of the Japanese will be shattered forever (try Kamiya Bar in Asakusa and you'll see what I mean). Head out to the countryside and things become slow, laid back and anything but high-tech. Here, it's the changing of the seasons that still dictates the flow of life for many.

Over the last decade or so, I've been fortunate to have traveled to almost every prefecture of the country, from the wilds of Hokkaido in the far north to the sun-kissed Okinawan islands way down south. I'm also fortunate to be able to earn a living by writing about the many facets of Japan, be that in books related to travel and culture or features on business and sustainability. But even now, Japan regularly finds new ways of surprising and re-energizing me. Sometimes it is something as simple as stumbling upon an old neighborhood for the first time on a walk around Tokyo or finding an exquisite temple garden in Kyoto. Sometimes it is just a fleeting conversation with a stranger. On occasions it's the familiar things that leave me smiling: nursery school kids getting wheeled around in giant laundry trolleys or the way any conversation with someone aged over 80 seems to begin with them telling me their age and proclaiming how active they still are.

I hope this book will help you find your own unforgettable Japan experiences. Happy travels.

Rob Goss

CONTENTS

Japan at a Glance

Geography

Situated in Eastern Asia, east of the Korean Peninsula and between the Sea of Japan and the North Pacific Ocean, the Japanese archipelago totals 364,485 square kilometers (140,728 square miles) of land spread over 6,852 islands. The four major islands are Hokkaido in the north; the centrally situated main island of Honshu, which is home to Tokyo, Kyoto, Osaka and Nagoya; Kyushu off the western end of Honshu; and Shikoku to the south of central Honshu.

Shinkyo-bashi in Nikko

Climate

With the Japanese archipelago stretching more than 3,000 km (1,864 miles) from southern tip to far north, the weather can range from subtropical in Okinawa to near Siberian in winter in central and northern Hokkaido. Between those extremes the climate remains similar: Honshu, Shikoku and Kyushu are hot and humid in summer with temperatures typically above 30 degrees Celsius; mostly warm, sunny and dry in autumn and spring (except for a short pre-summer rainy season and post-summer typhoon season); and in winter mostly dry but with temperatures dropping only into single digits away from the mountains.

People

At last count, in 2017, Japan's population was 126 million, of which around 35 million live in the Greater Tokyo area comprised of Tokyo and the neighboring prefectures of Chiba, Kanagawa and Saitama. Approximately 98.5% of the population is Japanese; the rest is made up primarily of Korean (5%) and Chinese (4%). The Japanese are the longest-living people in the world with an average life expectancy of 84.19 years (80.85 for men

Thatched buildings at Oshino with Mount Fuji in the background

The annual Doburoku festival in Shirakawa-go

and 87.71 for women), yet the population is declining as the country also claims the world's second lowest birthrate.

Language

The official language of Japan is Japanese. Besides Japanese, Okinawa has its own related but minor Ryukyuan languages, while the indigenous Ainu people of Hokkaido have the unrelated Ainu language. Japanese is the first language of 99% of the Japanese population, and with three separate writing systems (kanji, hiragana and katakana) that between them use thousands of different characters, not to mention a complex system of honorifics, it isn't the easiest language to quickly get to grips with. Not that you need to worry. In the main cities and tourist areas, you will be able to get by in English. Head out into the countryside, however, and you won't want to forget your phrasebook. To help make the language barriers a little less daunting, a survival guide to Japanese is included on pages 122–4, which covers useful expressions and pronunciation.

Religion

Because of the traditional rituals used for birth and death, the Japanese often say that they are born Shinto but die Buddhist. In fact, it's easier to consider the two religions as forming one set of traditional practices rather than being separate or conflicting faiths. Some 84% of Japanese say they practice traditions related to Shintoism, the indigenous religion of Japan, while 71% practice those related to Buddhism, which arrived from China in the 6th century. However, the Japanese don't typically consider themselves to be religious: more than 80% profess no religious affiliation and about 65% don't believe in God or Buddha.

Government

Japan is a parliamentary government with a constitutional monarchy, the current constitution having been adopted in 1947. Emperor Akihito is the chief of state, while the prime minister, as of writing Shinzo Abe, is the head of state. The legislative branch of government, the Diet, consists of a 242-member House of Councilors and a 450-member House of Representatives. The prime minister is designated by the Diet, and is usually the leader of the majority party or majority coalition in the House of Representatives.

MAKING THE MOST OF YOUR VISIT

For most visitors, Japan begins with **Tokyo**. But where do you start in a city that has so much to offer? If jetlag wakes you before sunrise the first morning, go straight to **Tsukiji Market** (page 11), where the frenetic market and great sushi will jolt you into life like a triple espresso. After that, take to the streets of nearby **Ginza** for its famed department stores, boutiques and high-end restaurants.

The next day, explore the city's old east side, starting with **Senso-ji Temple** in **Asakusa** (page 9) before moving to the **Ueno** district (page 29) for several of the city's best museums and Ueno Park. On day three, take in the magnificent **Meiji Jingu Shrine** (page 33) and neighboring **Yoyogi Park** before a change of pace among the teenyboppers of **Harajuku** and the fashionistas of **Omotesando-dori** (page 32). Another day could be spent first browsing the electronics and *otaku* (geek subculture) stores in **Akihabara** (page 28), then plunging into the crowded streets of **Shinjuku** (page 33)—the epitome of brash, modern Tokyo—or the more stylish **Roppongi Hills** and **Tokyo Midtown** urban developments in **Roppongi** (page 10).

Whatever you do, don't limit yourself to Tokyo, as mesmerizing as the city can be. Make an effort to get out of the capital and discover the incredible diversity of the rest of Japan. If time is limited, opt for a day trip to **Kamakura** (page 36), the 13th-century capital, and take in the **Daibutsu** (Great Buddha) at Hase's **Kotoku-in Temple** (page 12). With a little more time available, head a couple of hours north to the World Heritage **Tosho-gu Shrine** in **Nikko** (page 13), the outrageously lavish complex built by Tokugawa Ieyasu, the man who united Japan and became the first shogun of the Edo era. Consider combining that with a night at a traditional Japanese inn, or *ryokan*. Alternatively, take a train just under two hours west to **Hakone** (page 39) for a soak in one of the area's many natural outdoor hot springs and for superb views of majestic **Mount Fuji** (page 14).

The Shinkansen train tracks have been extended to the seaside city of **Kanazawa** (page 42), notable for its castle grounds and adjacent park, **Kenroku-en** (page 16), formerly the estate of the castle's Lord Maeda. The city boasts some of Japan's most delectable seafood in its famous Omi-cho market. The Japan Sea coastal area also is noted for its many hot springs, such as the **Yamashiro Onsen** (page 45), tempting for fans in need of a little luxurious bathing.

The **Japan Alps** are Japan's backbone, with the country's highest peaks, famed for their beauty, varied woods, wild flowers and, of course, snow. The nation has hundreds of serious mountain climbing groups, so trails exist over the three ranges, but the paths across the lower foothills lure thousands of ordinary citizens during the hot summer months. The centuries-old post towns of **Nakasendo** (page 98) are sprinkled along ancient paths traversing the steep terrain, a reminder of the once rugged lifestyles of the inhabitants of these steep valleys. Old inns that served as way stations for travelers now serve the modern hiker who emerges from the surrounding woodlands in search of a little sustenance. **Kamikochi** (page 98) is a 1,500-meter (4,900-foot) highland national park with nature trails and a campground with access to higher peaks. The narrow roads and deep winter snows close the area between mid-November and the end of March, but when open, the pristine air and alpine setting are absolutely addictive.

Better still, try to schedule at least a week exploring other parts of the country, starting with a few days in the former capital of **Kyoto** (page 47), the cultural yin to Tokyo's modern yang. The city's 17 **World Heritage Sites** include the decadently gilded temple of **Kinkaku-ji** (page 17) and the contrasting simplicity of **Ryoan-ji Temple**'s dry landscape garden (page 50). Kyoto also makes a good base for exploring other important sites in the **Kansai** region, for example, a day trip to the ancient temples of **Nara** (page 54), Japan's capital before Kyoto, or **Osaka** (page 56), Japan's second largest city. Looking farther afield, you could use Kyoto as a staging post en route to the atmospheric **Mount Koya** (page 23), home to some 120 monasteries of the Shingon sect of Buddhism.

If you still have time, extend your trip to **Shikoku** (page 62) for two or three days to visit the splendid **Dogo hot springs**, **Matsuyama Castle** and artistic **Naoshima Island**'s stunning array of contemporary art galleries and outdoor art installations (page 21). From Shikoku, it's an easy trip to **Hiroshima** (page 61) for the **Peace Memorial Park** (page 22)— the moving memorial at the site of the first nuclear attack—and the famous floating *torii*, or shrine gate, at **Itsukushima Shrine**. From there, move on to **Kyushu** (page 65) for a soak in the famed **Beppu hot springs**, and continue on to the southern island of **Yakushima** (page 24), with its ancient towering cedars.

The extreme north and south of Japan are equally worthwhile. **Hokkaido** (page 69), the large northern island shaped by its harsh winters, is not surprisingly home to Japan's premier ski slopes, in **Niseko** (page 25), where perfect powder snow attracts skiers from around the world. If you go, make sure to spend a night in **Sapporo** (page 67), Hokkaido's main city, to indulge in its wonderfully hearty cuisine and laid-back vibe. At the opposite end of the archipelago, in the far south, **Okinawa** (page 71) is the perfect place to end your trip, unwinding on its pristine beaches or diving amid its beautiful coral reefs.

HOW TO USE THIS BOOK

In the front of the book, we give you a brief overview of Japan, including its geography, climate, people, language, religion and government. **Chapter 1** covers Japan's "Don't Miss" Sights, detailing the top 18 places to visit and things to do, from staying at a temple on sacred Mount Koya to exploring the contemporary art galleries of Naoshima Island to skiing the perfect powder snow in Niseko on the northern island of Hokkaido.

In **Chapter 2**, we take a more detailed look at the varied regions and major cities that make up Japan, starting with the ultramodern, unerringly traditional and at times quirky faces of the capital Tokyo and ending up on the subtropical islands of Okinawa in the far south. In between, we explore several not-to-miss areas within day-trip range of Tokyo, including the ancient shrines and temples of Kamakura and the popular weekend retreat of Hakone, before heading west to the Japan Sea coast and the city of Kanazawa. The isolation of the mountains that one crosses between Tokyo and the Japan Sea Coast are home to a number of very picturesque towns. We then move on to Kyoto, the former capital and for many the cultural and spiritual heart of Japan. We also delve into Osaka, Japan's vibrant second city, and then the major islands of Kyushu and Shikoku.

The last section of the book is **Chapter 3**, Author's Recommendations. Here, we present some of Japan's better known hotels and restaurants, top kid-friendly activities, must-do activities in the great outdoors, must-see galleries and museums, and more. Lastly, the **Travel Tips** section presents all you need to know before you go, including the lowdown on visas, health and safety advice, important points of etiquette, essential Japanese, and much more to help take the stress out of your trip.

While all information is correct at time of print, do make sure to check ahead if you plan to visit any of the venues listed in this guide, as some places frequently change management, especially in cities that change as often and as rapidly as Tokyo and Osaka. Prices change, too, and occasionally senior discounts are available. Repair work may necessitate closing a venue. It is advisable to ask your hotel to check. As such, the publisher cannot accept responsibility for any errors that may be contained within the Travel Pack.

CHAPTER 1
JAPAN'S "Don't Miss" Sights

Ask anyone who has visited Japan to recommend a "must see" or "must do" list for your trip and you will get a variety of responses that underscores the diversity of the country. Some will tell you to go straight to the ancient temples of Kyoto or lace up your walking boots for the breathtaking natural scenery of the Japan Alps. Others will suggest you dive head first into Tokyo's old east end. The 18 listings that follow are a selection of Japan's "Don't Miss" Sights, chosen to offer a mix of the traditional and the ultramodern, the tranquil and the intense, the sacred and the cutting edge—components that combine to make Japan such a wonderfully distinctive and indelibly memorable experience.

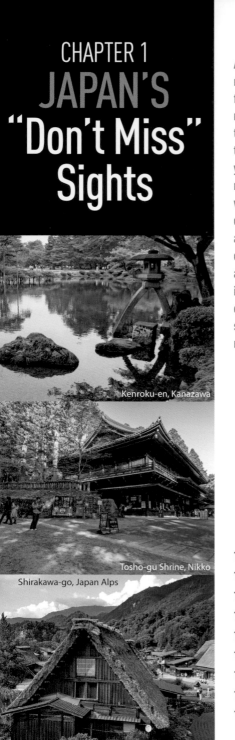

Kenroku-en, Kanazawa

Tosho-gu Shrine, Nikko

Shirakawa-go, Japan Alps

1 Senso-ji Temple, Tokyo

A journey to the heart of Old Tokyo's Asakusa district

Senso-ji Temple in **Asakusa** splits opinion. For some it's a tourist trap, for others it's the highlight of a visit to Tokyo. In truth, it can be both. The colorful **Nakamise-dori**, the shop-lined street that forms the main approach to Senso-ji, is as touristy as it gets in Tokyo with its plastic samurai swords, trinkets and slow-moving horde of tourists. The rest of the Senso-ji Temple complex is simply magnificent.

According to legend, there has been a temple here since the 620s, when two brothers snagged a golden image of Kannon, the goddess of mercy, in their nets while fishing in the nearby Sumida River. Awestruck by the tiny statue, they were inspired to build a temple in which to enshrine it, and Senso-ji was born. As Senso-ji's power grew over the centuries with the support first of the Kamakura imperial court and later of the Tokugawa shogunate, so too Asakusa grew around it, expanding from an insignificant fishing village to a thriving merchant town and then the city's premier entertainment district in the prewar years (page 29). Throughout, Senso-ji has always remained at Asakusa's heart and it's not hard to see why.

Senso-ji greets visitors with the great **Kaminari-mon** (Thunder Gate), a roofed gate standing almost 12 meters (39 feet) high and 12 meters wide under which hangs a 1,500-pound (680-kilogram) red paper lantern that itself measures some 4 meters (12 feet) in height. Protected on either side by the menacing bronze statues of Raijin and Fujin (the gods of thunder and wind), Kaminari-mon is the first of several imposing structures in the complex. At the other end of Nakamise-dori, the two-story **Hozomon Gate** stands 22 meters (72 feet) high and is decorated with three giant lanterns and two 800-pound (362-kilogram) straw sandals. Used to store many of Senso-ji's most precious relics, it is guarded by two identical 5-meter (16-foot)-tall statues of Nio, the guardian deity of the Buddha—two statues that make Raijin and Fujin look positively friendly. Beyond that, in air heavy with pungent incense, comes a five-tiered pagoda and the larger, albeit less ornate main building, in front of which visitors pray and wave incense smoke over themselves for its supposed curative powers.

Is it touristy? In parts, yes. But in the middle of a city as modern and short on space as Tokyo, it's a combination of tradition and scale that you shouldn't miss.

Opening Times Open all year round. **Getting There** Senso-ji is several minutes walk from Asakusa on the Asakusa and Ginza subway lines. **Contact** Senso-ji Temple: senso-ji.jp **Admission Fee** Free.

2 Roppongi Hills and Tokyo Midtown
The capital at its most modern and most stylish

Not much more than two decades ago, **Roppongi** was the preserve of late night drinkers and restaurant goers, just another drab piece of urbanity that would come to life (often raucously so) after dark. How things have changed! Today, with two of the city's most fashionable urban redevelopments, it's the epitome of cosmopolitan Tokyo.

The catalyst for change was billionaire Minoru Mori, head of the giant Mori Building Company, and the $2.5 billion **Roppongi Hills** complex he launched to much hype and success in 2003: the crowds that flocked to the complex in the first few months after it opened made Shibuya Crossing look sedate.

With more than 200 shops, boutiques, restaurants, cafés and bars, as well as the sleek Grand Hyatt Hotel, the stunningly contemporary **Mori Art Museum** (page 106) located on the top floors of the complex's glistening main tower, plus, in separate buildings, the headquarters of Asahi TV and some of the city's most exclusive apartments, it was rightly billed as a "city within a city," breaking new ground for Tokyo with its scale and luxury. It set the stage for other sleek urban developments that would soon follow, one of which would be built very near by.

Not to be outdone by Mori, Mitsui Fudosan, Japan's largest real estate developer, built a city within a city of its own—**Tokyo Midtown**—just down the road. Opened in 2007, Mitsui's complex is made up of five buildings and a central tower that, at 248 meters (814 feet), is the tallest building in Tokyo Prefecture. Its five-story **Galleria** is home to 73,000 square meters (790,000 square feet) of stores and restaurants, while the surrounding grounds include a spacious park and garden.

Where Roppongi Hills boasts the Grand Hyatt, Midtown has the five-star Ritz Carlton (page 79) on the upper floors of its main tower. Midtown doesn't do badly for art either, with the **Design Sight 21_21** (2121designsight.jp) gallery and workshop, created by renowned architect Tadao Ando and fashion designer Issey Miyake to showcase modern Japanese design, as well as the **Suntory Museum of Art** (suntory.com/sma) with its fine collection of traditional Japanese art. The result is two cities within a city, standing face to face and creating the quintessential Tokyo experience.

Opening Times Varies by store, attraction and restaurant, but most places within Roppongi Hills and Midtown will be open by 11 a.m. Check the websites below. **Getting There** Roppongi Station is on the Hibiya and Oedo subway lines. **Contact** Roppongi Hills: roppongihills.com. Tokyo Midtown: tokyo-midtown.com **Admission Fee** Free

3 Tokyo's Tsukiji Market

Energetic tuna auctions and the city's best sushi breakfast

It's 5.30 a.m. and Tokyo's **Tsukiji Market** bursts into life with the ringing of a bell that heralds the start of the daily tuna auctions. What follows is a blur of hand signals set to a cacophony of hollers, a rapid to and fro between auctioneer and wholesalers that's incomprehensible to the outsider. It's like watching a classical performance, but with choreographed *kabuki* moves and with kimono replaced by rubber boots and overalls. And instead of a theater, you are in a cavernous warehouse filled with line upon line of whole frozen tunas.

Away from the auction, the sprawling main market is a hive of activity all through the morning, with more than 60,000 wholesalers, buyers and shippers busy supplying the city's restaurants and shops with what amounts to more than 700,000 tons of seafood a year. To put that into context, each day in excess of ¥1.5 billion ($19 million) worth of produce is traded here, and not only seafood. Tsukiji, or Tokyo Metropolitan Central Wholesale Market to give its proper name, also trades in vegetables, meat and even cooking utensils, while the outer public market teems with small sushi bars.

What the original fishermen of Tsukiji would make of it now is anyone's guess. The area was nothing more than mud flats when the first Edo-era shogun, Tokugawa Ieyasu, brought the fisherman in from Osaka at the start of the 17th century with the order to supply his new capital with seafood. Not until after the Great Kanto Earthquake of 1923 and the subsequent consolidation of small private markets into large wholesale venues did Tsukiji takes its current form.

Tsukiji reigns as the world's largest fish market, but that looks set to end. The Metropolitan Government of Tokyo is planning to move the fish auction market to a new (and controversial) site in eastern Tokyo in order to cash in on the land value of Tsukiji's current location, which is estimated to be 350 billion yen or approximately 5 million yen per *tsubo* (3.3 square meters). However, the outer market precincts with their food stalls and sushi restaurants will remain.

Opening Times The fish auction market is open from 5 a.m to 3 p.m. The tuna auctions are limited to 120 people on a first-come basis and begin at 5.25 a.m. Closed Sunday and 2nd/4th Weds. The outer market and sushi restaurants are open all day. **Getting There** Tsukiji Shijo Station is on the Oedo subway line and Tsukiji Station is on the Hibiya subway line. The market is a short walk from either. **Admission Fee** Free. **Important** While the outer market and sushi restaurants will remain at the current location, the fish auction market may move to a new site in Toyosu sometime in the future but the date has not yet been decided upon.

4 The Great Buddha at Kamakura
Japan's most serene and storied religious figure

With a smile as enigmatic as the Mona Lisa's and a face that has appeared on almost as many postcards as Mount Fuji, the giant statue of **Buddha** at **Hase**, near **Kamakura** (page 36), is one of Japan's most recognizable sights. It is also one of the most worthwhile places to visit within day-trip distance of Tokyo.

Plenty of history has unfolded during the 750 years the Daibutsu has held court on its stone pedestal at **Kotoku-in Temple**, where he serenely sits cross-legged, eyes gently closed in meditation. The Muromachi, Momoyama, Edo, Meiji, Taisho and Showa eras have come and gone, as too have numerous wars and natural disasters. In fact, it was because of one of the latter that the Daibutsu is now exposed to the elements, for the wooden building that once housed him was washed away by a tsunami in 1495, a frightening thought given that Kotoku-in is almost a kilometer (half a mile) inland. Yet other than turning his bronze finish into its distinctive streaky mix of gray, green and soft metallic blue, the years exposed to the sun, wind and rain have been kind to the Daibutsu. The only real damage he has suffered is losing the gold leaf coating that some believe he may have had when he was completed in 1252.

Although tourists primarily come (at times in droves) to see the giant Buddha, the rest of Hase is also worth exploring. **Hase-dera**, a temple high on the hillside between Kotoku-in and Hase Station, contains a 9-meter (30-foot)-tall gilded wooden statue of Kannon, said to have washed ashore at Hase after being carved and tossed into the sea by a monk from Nara during the 8th century. Nearby is **Yuigahama Beach**, a peaceful weekday spot with broad ocean views that's ideal for a picnic away from the worst of Kotoku-in's crowds. And just a few stations away are the historic temples and shrines of Kamakura (page 36), Japan's capital in the 13th century, which with an early start you can comfortably combine with Hase to make a great day trip from Tokyo.

Opening Times Open daily 8 a.m. to at least 5 p.m.
Getting There Hase is three stops from Kamakura on the Enoden Line. Kamakura is best reached from Tokyo on the JR Yokosuka Line (via Yokohama) or on the JR Shonan-Shinjuku Line from Shinjuku or Shibuya. **Contact** Kotoku Temple: kotoku-in.jp
Admission Fee ¥200.

5 Tosho-gu Shrine, Nikko
A memorial to Japan's first shogun—in a stunning setting

Garish or grand? The **Tosho-gu Shrine** complex in **Nikko** (page 41) most definitely qualifies as both. Its Yomei-mon Gate (Sun Blaze Gate) is a riot of color adorned with 400 ornate carvings of dancing maidens, birds and flowers. Its deep red five-story pagoda is accented with intricate decorations and vivid golds and greens. The more serene white and gold of the Kara-mon Gate provides the backdrop for even more elaborate carvings.

An estimated 15,000 craftsmen took two years to build the Tosho-gu complex, during which they went through some 2.5 million sheets of gold leaf, a fitting decadence perhaps considering that the shrine was built for one of Japanese history's most towering figures—Tokugawa Ieyasu, the warlord who unified Japan at the start of the 17th century to become the first of the Edo-era shoguns.

Yet Tosho-gu isn't all about Edo-era ostentation. Its natural setting, amid an ancient cryptomeria forest, evokes a sense of calm. And away from the glare of the main shrine buildings, Tosho-gu boasts many subtle points of interest. Above the shrine's sacred stables, which shelter a beautiful white imperial horse

given to Japan by New Zealand, hangs a famed carving of the three wise monkeys—remember "Hear no evil, Speak no evil, See no evil"?—an image that represents the three main principles of Tendai Buddhism. Nearby, en route to Ieyasu's surprisingly understated tomb, is the equally renowned (though so small it's easily missed) 16th- or 17th-century Nemuri Neko carving of a sleeping cat.

Just as impressive is the Honji-do, a small hall that is actually part of a separate temple, not Tosho-gu. The hall's ceiling is adorned with the painting of a raging dragon that the temple's priests bring to life by standing directly under its head and clapping two blocks of wood together, thus creating an echo that shrieks dramatically through the temple.

Opening Times Open daily from 8 a.m. to at least 4 p.m. **Getting There** Nikko is best reached on the Tobu Line (Tobu Nikko Station) from Asakusa in Tokyo (2 hours 10 minutes). From there frequent buses make the short run to Tosho-gu, which is otherwise a 20-minute walk. **Contact** Nikko Tourist Association: nikko-jp.org **Admission Fee** Admission to Tosho-gu is ¥1,300, but to see all of Nikko's main attractions it's better to buy a ¥1,000 combination ticket permitting entrance to Tosho-gu (Ieyasu's tomb then costs an additional ¥520) and the nearby Futarasan and Rinno-ji temples.

6 Mount Fuji and Hakone
Japan's most iconic sight, now a World Heritage Site

Whether you catch a fleeting glimpse of the near perfectly symmetrical dome through a train window or watch in wonder from Tokyo as her snow-capped peak appears far to the west through the city smog, there's something mesmerizing about **Mount Fuji** (known in Japanese as Fuji-san).

Maybe it's the way Fuji-san dominates the vista as she straddles the prefectures of Yamanashi and Shizuoka. At 3,776 meters (12,388 feet), she is comfortably the nation's tallest peak, and with no other mountains nearby, Fuji-san stands fully visible from sprawling base to narrowing peak. Her influence on Japan has been profound. The peak has inspired countless artists and integrated herself into both Shinto and Buddhist traditions. The legendary *ukiyo-e* woodblock printmaker Hokusai (1760–1849) was so smitten that he dedicated much of his work to capturing Fuji's changing moods. His woodblock series, *36 Views of Mount Fuji*, includes the celebrated *Great Wave Off Kanagawa*, whose snow-capped Fuji in the distance and giant foaming wave menacingly poised to break in the foreground is recognizable to anyone with a passing interest in Japan.

In Shintoism, the peak of the now dormant volcano is home to a fire god and, despite its naked lunarscape, a goddess of trees. In Buddhism, Fuji is home to Dainichi Nyorai, the Buddha of All-Illuminating Wisdom. Consequently, pilgrims have journeyed to Fuji's peak for spiritual enlightenment for centuries. Fuji-san's symbolic power was reputedly even recognized by the Allied authorities in World War II. According to one tale, they planned to bomb Fuji's white cap with blood red paint in order to break the Japanese spirit.

The best way to enjoy Fuji-san up close is to visit the **Hakone** area (page 39), a popular weekend retreat for Tokyoites because of its natural hot springs, fine inns, mountain vistas and an array of other attractions, including the brilliant **Hakone Open Air Museum** (page 107) and the volcanic **Owakudani Valley** with its steaming sulfur vents and hot springs.

If you want a really close look at Fuji, you can even climb it in the summer months, although it is a long challenging hike. However, you don't need to venture out of Tokyo to get a good view. On a clear day, head up to the free observation deck on the 45th floor of Tokyo Metropolitan Government building in Shinjuku (page 34) and Fuji-san reveals all her wonder.

Getting There The Hakone area is served by Hakone-Yumoto Station, which can be reached on the Odakyu Line from Shinjuku Station in Tokyo in 80 minutes. **Contact** Hakone Town Tourist Association: hakone.or.jp/english

7 Traditional Houses of Shirakawa-go
Head back in time to the villages of the Hida Highlands

Seeing **Ogimachi village** for the first time, it's easy to imagine you are looking upon a scene unchanged for centuries. The village is one of several in the Shirakawa-go region in the Hida Highlands (page 46) that is still dominated by towering thatched farmhouses that blend with a carpet of lush green rice paddies and a backdrop of dense forest to create a scene that could be straight from a Brothers' Grimm tale. There's good reason these villages have barely changed over the centuries. Less than a hundred years ago, the densely forested valleys here were among the most secluded in Japan. Heavy snowfall and a lack of road connections left the area's villages cut off from modernization.

The *gassho-zukuri* name given to the farmhouses comes from their sloping A-shaped roofs. Designed much like those in Scandinavia to stop snow accumulating in the harsh winter months, they are said to resemble hands in prayer (*gassho*). The distinctive thatched houses also reveal much about the traditional lifestyle of the area. Sometimes reaching up to five floors in height, they can house several generations of a family, and in some cases more than a single family, and allow enough space for indoor cultivation. Taking advantage of the heat rising from the living quarters down below, often the upper floors are used for the raising of silkworms.

All seasons provide a stunning backdrop to these isolated mountain villages. Because of the highly flammable nature of the structures, on the last Sunday in October the local fire departments hose down the straw roofs after the parching sun of summer. In winter, when the roofs seem to support more snow than it is possible, the interiors are lighted and snow-covered pathways are lantern-lit to allow visitors to carefully wend their way and imagination into a lifestyle that is virtually unthinkable, a time when people lived merely inside, a few degrees warmer than outside.

Ainokura, another *gasho-zukuri* village, is about an hour's ride north with fewer homes but also far fewer tourists. The setting is just as majestic but access is less convenient.

Getting There Shirakawa-go can be accessed via Nagoya, from where it is just over 2 hours on the JR Takayama Line to Takayama Station. Buses that run to Shirakawa-go take 50 minutes. Also accessed by a 90-minute bus ride from Kanazawa. See online timetable: japan-guide.com/bus/shirakawa-go.html **Contact** Shirakawa Village Office: shirakawa-go.org/english

8 Kanazawa Castle and Kenroku-en
A traditional castle town on Japan's western shore

All that glitters in this city is gold, a city whose wealth was dug out of the gold mines of Sado Island and put to good use arming one of Japan's most powerful clans. Pre-modern cities were built around her temples, shrines, ports and castles. **Kanazawa** (page 42) is one of Japan's best examples of a castle town with its scattering of warrior homes and the artisans who provided objects of beauty for its residents.

A new Shinkansen train barrels into Kanazawa Station from Tokyo in two and a half hours, bringing an infusion of tourists and their appetites. The station and its massive glass and steel dome displays a unique hand-crafted wooden gate that resembles a traditional hand drum.

Located on a slight rise in the center of the city, **Kanazawa Castle** offers a view of Lord Maeda's domain and the ridge of mountains that foiled any attack upon his well-armed and faithful warriors. The castle walls are a sparkling white, matching the snowy peaks in the distance a good five months of the year.

Lord Maeda's wealth came not only from its gold reserves but also from ship-ping. The port provided the townspeople with many of the refined goods that came from Kyoto, carrying back the sea products that abound in these waters.

The garden that adjoins Kanazawa Castle is ranked as one of the top three gardens of Japan. Opened to the public in 1874, **Kenroku-en** is expansive and beautifully maintained, with glorious ponds and some of the most pampered pine trees one will find anywhere. The seasonal floral display is well depicted on the information board inside.

Speaking of the rich bounty of seafood lavished upon its citizens, Kanazawa's **Omi-cho market** is a kaleidoscope of color, aromas and tastes, capable of pleasing everyone who wishes to sample the delicacies on display in its busy shops.

Kanazawa Castle Park Open 9 a.m. to 4.30 p.m. year round. **Getting There** A 5-minute walk from the Kenrokuen bus stop or a 15-minute bus ride from Kanazawa JR Station. **Contact** www.pref. ishikawa.jp/siro-niwa/kanazawajou/ **Admission Fee** ¥310; children ¥100; over 65 years of age free. **Kenroku-en Park** Open 7 a.m. to 6 p.m. **Getting There** Take the Loop Line bus from Kanazawa Station. **Contact** pref.ishikawa.jp/siro-niwa/ Kenroku-en/index.html/ **Admission Fee** ¥310

9 Kinkaku-ji Temple, Kyoto
The quintessential "Golden Pavilion" of historic Kyoto

Few sights in Japan are as iconic as the golden reflection of **Kinkaku-ji** (Temple of the Golden Pavilion) shimmering on the still waters of Kyoko-chi (Mirror Pond) that heightens its beauty.

The pure gold leaf coating the top two floors of the three-story building is what sends the hordes of visitors to Kinkaku-ji into a photographic frenzy, but pause a while to study the structure and you notice that there is far more to Kinkaku-ji than its gilding. Each floor is in a different but complementary architectural style. The first is in the *shinden-zukuri* style common to Heian (11th-century) imperial aristocracy; the second in the style of warrior aristocrats, or *buke-zukuri*; and the third in traditional Chinese *cha'an* style.

As stunning a sight as Kinkaku-ji is, many visitors are surprised to learn that the temple building is actually a modern reconstruction. The original, built in 1397 as part of a retirement villa for shogun Ashikaga Yoshimitsu and then converted into a Zen temple upon his death, was burned to the ground by a young monk (whose possible motives and internal strife were the subject of Yukio Mishima's 1956 novel, *Temple of the Golden Pavilion*) in 1950. By 1955 it had been rebuilt except for the gilding, which was eventually restored in 1987.

Kinkaku-ji's rise from the ashes was crowned in 1994 when the temple was deservedly granted World Heritage status along with 16 other sites in Kyoto. The fire-loving monk didn't enjoy a similarly happy end. As Kinkaku-ji burned around him, he botched an attempt to commit suicide and was sentenced to seven years in jail. He died of tuberculosis in 1956 shortly after his early release for medical reasons.

Opening Times Daily from 9 a.m to 5 p.m.
Getting There From Kyoto Station take bus number 101 or 205 to the Kinkaku-ji Michi bus stop or take bus number 59 or 12 to the Kinkaku-ji Mae bus stop. **Contact** Kinkaku-ji Temple: shokoku-ji.jp
Admission Fee ¥400

10 Kyoto's Kiyomizu Temple
Refined beauty in perfect harmony with its surroundings

Few places in Kyoto are as pretty or better illustrate the deeply entwined relationship between Japanese culture and nature than **Kiyomizu Temple**.

By day, the temple's main hall, the **Hondo**, is set against a rich natural backdrop that changes with each season: pink hues of cherry blossom in spring, lush greens in summer, earthy reds and yellows in autumn, and the occasional white tint on naked branches in winter. By night, when many of the temple's buildings are illuminated and lanterns accent the shop-lined **Chawan-zaka** slope that leads visitors up toward the complex, Kiyomizu's three-storied pagoda bathes the area in a soft orange glow. Whenever you visit, it's captivatingly beautiful.

Built on a rock face that overlooks a small valley, the Hondo is Kiyomizu's star attraction, its protruding wooden veranda one of the classic images of Kyoto. It used to be said that anyone who leapt from the overhanging veranda and survived the 13-meter (43-foot) fall unscathed would have his or her dreams answered; those who died would be rewarded by sainthood. No doubt seen as a win-win situation by some, jumping became such a problem during the Edo era that in 1872 the government outlawed the act.

A far nicer tale awaits beyond the Hondo, at **Jishu Jinja**, a shrine partially dedicated to a deity of love and a good marriage. In front of the shrine are two "love stones" set 6 meters (20 feet) apart. It is said that if you can walk between the two stones, eyes closed, you will one day find true love (some interpretations say you may already have found it). Stray from the path, however, and the romantic news is not so good—but at least you'll have the glorious sight of Kiyomizu to console you.

The grounds of the temple lead to a fountain that allows visitors a taste of its therapeutic spring waters. Long-handled dippers allow one to catch a ladle full. The grounds go downhill from here, into a forested area and eventually to Kyoto's largest cemetery, **Toribeno**, with 90,000 graves. The living and departed citizens still maintain a spectacular view of the ancient city.

Opening Times Main hall is open daily from 6 a.m. to 6 p.m. **Getting There** Head to either the Kiyomizu-michi or Gojo-zaka bus stop served by buses 100, 202, 206 or 207 from Kyoto Station. **Contact** Kiyomizu Temple: kiyomizudera.or.jp **Admission Fee** Main hall ¥300.

11 Horyu-ji Temple, Nara
The world's oldest wooden building, founded in 607

To choose just one of Nara's many ancient temples for special attention is a hard task. One could opt for **Todai-ji Temple** (todaiji.or.jp), a World Heritage Site that houses a 15-meter (49-foot)-high bronze statue of Buddha in one of the largest wooden buildings in the world. Or there is **Kofuku-ji Temple** (kohfukuji.com) and its 600-year-old five-story pagoda, the original of which was moved here from Kyoto, 35 km (19 miles) to the north, in the 8th century.

But in the city that many Japanese consider the birthplace of Japanese civilization, indeed a city that was the country's pre-Kyoto capital from 710 to 784, the standout has to be the grand temple complex of **Horyu-ji**. Boasting the nation's oldest five-story pagoda, which remarkably was dismantled in World War II to protect it against Allied air raids and then reassembled with the same materials after the war, Horyu-ji is also home to the equally important **Kon-do** (Golden Hall), a building believed to have been built around 670, making it the world's oldest extant wooden building.

Horyu-ji was founded in 607, just 50 years after Buddhism first came to Japan, and its scale and splendor serve as a testament to how quickly and deeply the then recently imported religion rooted itself in Japan under the patronage of Prince Shotoku (574–622), the man who founded Horyu-ji. It was Horyu-ji that Shotoku used as a base from which to spread Buddhism across the country, and some of the earliest relics from that period of growth (some of Japanese Buddhism's most precious items) are still kept at Horyu-ji's Kon-do today.

These items include the original Medicine Buddha that Shotoku supposedly built Horyu-ji to hold and a bronze image of Buddha dated to 623. Yet the most revered of Horyu-ji's images is elsewhere, in the 8th-century **Yumedono** building in the complex's eastern precinct. This is the 178.8-cm (5 foot 10 inch)-high statue thought to be a life-size replica of Prince Shotoku, and which for centuries was kept hidden from all under a white cloth, only finally being uncovered in 1884.

Opening Times Open daily from 8 a.m. to 4.30 p.m. **Getting There** Nara is 40 minutes from Kyoto on the Kintetsu-Kyoto Line's Limited Express and can also be reached by JR lines from Kyoto and Osaka. Buses run half hourly between Nara Station and Horyu-ji. **Contact** Horyu-ji Temple: horyuji.or.jp **Admission Fee** Horyu-ji ¥1,500; Kofuku-ji ¥300.

12 Himeji Castle
The archetypal "White Heron" samurai fortress

Of the 142 castles dotted around Japan, none can quite match the majestic **Himeji-jo**, 50 kilometers (28 miles) west of Kobe. Just ask Hollywood. The distinctive white plaster façade and gray *kawara* roof tiles of Himeji-jo's five-story main tower (the Tenshukaku) and its three smaller donjons have provided a quintessentially Japanese backdrop for *The Last Samurai* and the Sean Connery-era Bond film *You Only Live Twice*.

Originally built in the mid-14th century, then restored and added to on several occasions over the following three centuries, this imposing collection of keeps and turrets has been likened to a heron spreading its wings, earning the castle the nickname Hakuro-jo (White Heron Castle). But it's a heron both cunning and virtually impossible to breach. Originally, the castle had three moats, 84 gates and a maze of narrow, zigzagging passages designed to disorient attackers while defending forces could fire upon them through the safety of 1,000 "loophole" firing windows.

As one might expect of a structure that dominates Himeji's skyline, the castle is a focal point for many of the city's main annual events. The Himeji Castle Cherry Blossom Viewing Fair and Princess Senhime Peony Festival in spring, the Himeji Castle Festival in summer, and the Moon Viewing Fair and Himeji All Japan Ceramics Market in autumn are all held on its grounds.

Alongside Himeji-jo's moats you will find the splendid **Koko-en Gardens**, a collection of nine linked Edo-style gardens built in 1992, while within a short walk are two stunning examples of modern architecture: Kenzo Tange's **Hyogo Prefectural Museum of History** and Tadao Ando's **Museum of Literature**. The former is a minimalist tour de force of concrete and glass cubes by the man many consider the godfather of modern Japanese architectural design. Tadao Ando is the force behind many of Naoshima's art galleries (page 21) and the Omotesando Hills urban development (page 31), and the Museum of Literature is an example of his finest work, combining rough concrete, water features and angular patterns, with Himeji's defining structure—the castle—providing the perfect backdrop.

Opening Times Open daily from 9 a.m. to at least 4 p.m. **Getting There** Himeji can be reached direct by train from Tokyo in 3 hours. From Osaka it's an hour on the JR Sanyo Line. The castle is a 15-minute walk from Himeji Station. **Contact** Himeji Castle: himeji-castle.gr.jp **Admission Fee** ¥600 (¥720 with combined Koko-en ticket)

13   Naoshima, Island of Art
Cutting-edge art installations on a beautiful island

Two decades ago, the Japanese publishing company Benesse Holdings and the Fukutake Foundation chose the picturesque island of **Naoshima** as the site for a project aimed at showcasing the best of Japanese and international contemporary art, including the iconic Yellow Pumpkin (pictured) by Yayoi Kusuma. The result has been a spectacular renaissance, transforming a sleepy fishing island into an undoubted high point on the country's art scene.

The **Benesse Art Site Naoshima (BASN) project** began in 1992 with the construction of the Tadao Ando-designed **Benesse House**, a strikingly sleek beachfront gallery and hotel that today includes in its collection pieces by David Hockney, Jackson Pollock and Andy Warhol. That would be impressive enough, but on the sun-kissed beaches and wooded hills that make up Benesse's grounds, there are also numerous outdoor art installations that for many visitors are the most memorable of Naoshima's artistic offerings.

BASN has also had a hand in the island's **Art House Project**, which began in 1998 and has seen a handful of the old wooden houses and an Edo-era shrine at the fishing village of Honmura converted into permanent art installations. Ando has also continued his involvement with Naoshima, designing the **Chichu Art Museum**, a cavernous concrete structure built into the island's southern hills that opened in 2004 and holds works by Claude Monet, Walter De Maria and James Turrell. More recently, he was involved with Naoshima's latest major gallery, the **Lee Ufan Museum**, dedicated to works by artist Lee Ufan.

Fans of the esteemed architect Tadao Ando should visit the **Ando Museum**, which features his signature use of unadorned concrete in a traditional 100-year-old wooden house, a fitting expression of his iconic architecture.

On Naoshima, there is art in unconventional locations as well. Inside and out, the island's fully functional public bathhouse, **I Love Yu** (*yu* means "hot water" in Japanese), is a riot of pop art, mosaics and erotica designed by Japanese artist Shinro Ohtake.

The Naoshima Art Project is now extended to two other islands, **Inujima** and **Teshima**, offering a stunning look at some of Japan's contemporary artists. Once on these islands, visitors, after paying an entrance fee to the art works, are free to walk around as they please. Against a backdrop of sea and sky, the airiness of the structures lifts the spirits, a soaring gesture into the future of art in Japan.

Getting There Ferries from Takamatsu (1 hour, ¥520) and Uno (an hour from Okayama; 20 minutes, ¥290) sail to Naoshima several times daily. Boats also go to Inujima and Teshima from Takamatsu on Shikoku and to Uno and Hoden on Honshu. **Contact** Benesse Art Site Naoshima: benesse-artsite. jp/en/ **Admission Fee** Admission to Teshima ¥1,540; Inujima ¥2,160; Chichu Art museum ¥2,060.

14 Hiroshima's Peace Memorial Park
A poignant memorial and a symbol of hope

Nothing has come to symbolize the horrors of nuclear war like the disfigured frame of the former Hiroshima Prefectural Industrial Hall. Situated in Hiroshima's Peace Memorial Park, the **Gempaku Dome** (its familiar name) serves as a vivid reminder of the destruction that befell the city on the morning of August 6, 1945, when the 4,400-kilogram (9,700-pound) nuclear payload of the B-29 Super-fortress bomber named "Enola Gay" annihilated central Hiroshima in a split second, claiming some 80,000 lives.

As a trip around the park's moving and in places harrowing museum reveals, that was just the start. Another 60,000 of Hiroshima's then 350,000 residents died of injuries in the days and weeks that followed. And some two-thirds of the city's structures were lost in the blast and ensuing firestorm, so it seems almost inconceivable that the dome, located in the bomb's hypocenter, could survive. In part that's why the Gempaku Dome speaks so poignantly to so many. It isn't just a testament to the horror of nuclear war, its survival against the odds has come to represent hope, perseverance and the indestructibility of the human spirit, the same qualities that saw Hiroshima rebuild from rubble to become a thriving modern city. It's impossible not to be moved when you stand before it.

The same can be said for many of the park's other sights, among which the most heartrending is the **Children's Peace Monument**, a 9-meter (30-foot)-high domed pedestal atop which a life-size bronze statue of a child holds aloft a giant paper crane. It is dedicated to 12-year-old Sadoko Sasaki, a leukemia patient in Hiroshima, who hoped she would be cured if she could fold 1,000 origami cranes, traditionally a symbol of health and longevity in Japan. Sadoko never got to 1,000, succumbing to her illness in 1955 before reaching her teenage years. Her classmates, however, continued to fold cranes for her and later successfully petitioned the nation to construct the Peace Monument in honor of Sadoko and the thousands of children whose lives were cut short by the blast. Thousands of schools around Japan contributed donations to fund the monument, and every year some 10 million cranes are sent here from around the world, some of which you'll see on display in glass cases surrounding it.

Opening Times Museum open daily from 8.30 a.m. to 5 p.m. **Getting There** Hiroshima can be reached by rail from Osaka, Kyoto and Tokyo. Hiro-shima Airport also has connections to Tokyo, Sapporo and Okinawa. **Contact** Hiroshima Peace Site: pcf.city. hiroshima.jp **Admission Fee** Admission to the museum is ¥200 for adults and ¥100 for students.

15 The Holy Mountain of Koya-san
Monastic life on one of Japan's most sacred sites

In 816, the Buddhist monk Kobo Daishi came upon **Mount Koya** (locally called Koya-san) while wandering the country in search of somewhere suitably meditative to establish a temple. One can only imagine what Koya-san was like then, but something about the densely wooded mountain must have resonated with Daishi because he chose Koya-san as the place to found the Shingon school of Buddhism. Today, some 120 Shingon monasteries cluster around the site of Daishi's first temple, attracting a steady stream of pilgrims and tourists to what has long been considered one of Japan's holiest mountains.

A first stop for many who make the journey south of Osaka, on train lines that gradually become more winding and remote before immersing themselves in thick woodland and verdant valleys, is **Okuno-in**. This vast wooded cemetery exudes an almost primeval atmosphere with its tall cedars, moss-covered stone stupas and small jizo statues dressed in vivid red bibs. At its eastern end, the cemetery gives way to a richly decorated hall lit by 10,000 constantly burning oil lanterns, the **Hall of Lanterns,** behind which, almost hidden in a cloud of incense and dense woodland, is Daishi's understated and off-limits mausoleum. Whether you are religious or not, the incense and droning chants of visiting pilgrims coming through the ancient wood create a powerful, electrifying energy.

Okuno-in is one of several reasons Koya-san received World Heritage status in 2004. On the other side of Koya-san, the Shingon sect's main temple, the **Kongobu-ji**, is another. Although not the most eye-catching of structures, it boasts a must-see collection of 16th-century screen paintings and one of the country's largest landscaped rock gardens, which, much like the one at Ryoan-ji in Kyoto (page 50), offers visitors a cryptic arrangement of rocks and raked gravel.

Rounding off the Koya-san experience is the accommodation. Approximately 50 of the monasteries offer *shukubo* (temple accommodation; see page 83), which typically features a Spartan and tranquil *tatami* mat guest room, a multicourse vegetarian dinner and the chance to join the monks and pilgrims for early morning prayers. If you are lucky, that will include being able to observe the morning fire ceremonies, during which a lone monk burns 108 small pieces of wood representative of the 108 defilements that must be overcome before reaching enlightenment. Accompanied by pulsating chanting and leaping flames, it's a spectacular way to start the day.

Getting There From Namba Station in Osaka, take the Nankai Line to Gokurakubashi Station (70–100 minutes; sometimes requiring a change at Hashimoto Station). From there it's a 5-minute cable car ride up to Koya-san. **Contact** Koya-san Tourist Association: eng.shukubo.net

16 Yakushima Island, Kyushu
A richly diverse ecosystem and World Heritage Site

If you are like the tens of thousands of Tokyoites who reach for face masks and antihistamines every spring, when cedar pollen floods in from the western hills, **Yakushima** may not be the most suitable of destinations. The small circular island, 30 kilometers (17 miles) in diameter and 1,000 kilometers (almost 600 miles) southwest of Tokyo, is famed for its giant, ancient cedars.

Dubbed the "Alps on the Ocean" for its 40 or so craggy peaks that reach upward of 1,000 meters (3,280 feet), providing the slopes on which the mighty cedars grow, Yakushima came to international attention when it was granted World Heritage status in 1993 because of its unique flora and fauna. That designation was made primarily because of the several thousand-year-old Yaku-sugi cedars (the eldest of which are claimed by some to be the oldest in the world at an estimated 7,200 years), but also for a rich diversity that includes the Yakushima rhododendron, which speckles the island pink, white and red in June.

Although it attracts Japanese tourists, Yakushima has so far remained off the beaten path for international travelers, which is remarkable given its stunning primeval beauty. The cedars tower above dense foliage that carpets an undulating sea of granite-rich mountains. Hiking trails cut across Tolkien-like mountain streams in subtropical rainforest that perspires a deep mossy aroma. Away from the interior, the rainforest gives way to a coastline of pristine beaches and offshore diving spots.

The island is a naturalist's dream, but it's not always easy on travelers. The heat and humidity can be oppressive, especially in July and August, while the island attracts so much rain—some 10 meters (33 feet) a year on average in the interior—that the 14,000 inhabitants wryly claim it to be the only place on earth to get 35 days of rain a month. But don't let that put you off. Yakushima will leave you wet but awestruck too.

Getting There There are daily flights to Yakushima's small airport from Kagaoshima and from Itami in Osaka. The island can also be reached from Kagoshima, 60 kilometers (33 miles) away, by hydrofoil (2 hours) and ferry (4 hours). **Contact** Kagoshima Prefectural Visitors Bureau: kagoshima-kankou.com

17 Niseko Ski Resort, Hokkaido
Japan's northern island has the world's best snow

The small ski resort town of **Niseko** in southwestern Hokkaido, in Japan's far north, lays claim to the finest powder snow in the world and volcanic alpine vistas to match; the 1,898-meter (6,227-foot)-high **Mount Yotei**, often likened to Mount Fuji for its symmetry, stands out among the clouds opposite the main slopes. The name Niseko is derived from the ethnic Ainu language of Hokkaido and is short for Niseko Annupura, which translates as the rather long-winded but apt "mountain with a river, which runs around the bottom of a sheer cliff."

After a 1970s boom that saw the area establish itself as a favorite among Japanese skiers, Niseko went into gradual decline, and the once fashionable hotels showed their age as skiers headed to newer destinations. In recent years, however, Niseko has risen again and it now boasts four interconnected resorts—Grand Hirafu, Hanazono, Niseko Village and Niseko Annupuri—that are up to international standards and finally do justice to the quality of the area's snow. In the process, Niseko has also become one of the most foreigner-friendly destinations in the country, in large part thanks to an influx of Australian property developers and tourists from Southeast Asia and China. Almost all the hotels, restaurants and ski schools offer English service, still something of a rarity in Japan outside major urban centers and major destinations like Kyoto.

The area also offers diversity. Away from the resorts in Niseko there are prime back-country powder and ample opportunities for ice climbing, telemark skiing and snowboarding through virgin snow. And when the ski season draws to a close in April (it starts in late November), the snow makes way for a summer season of whitewater rafting, mountain biking, hiking, golfing and kayaking. Add to that the year-round mineral-rich hot springs, perfect for soaking away your exertions, and it's no wonder Niseko is going through a renaissance.

Getting There From Sapporo Station, take the JR Kaisoku Airport (Rapid Service) to Otaru Station (45 minutes), then the JR Hakodate Line to Niseko Station (1 hour 40 minutes). Alternatively, buses run direct from Sapporo (approximately 3 hours). Numerous daily flights connect Sapporo's New Chitose Airport with Tokyo, Osaka and other major cities. **Contact** Niseko Promotion Board: nisekotourism.com/en

18 The Yaeyama Islands, Okinawa
Pristine nature and distinctive Ryukyuan culture

The **Yaeyama Islands** are as remote a place as you can find in Japan. At the southernmost and westernmost extremity of the country, this group of 10 islands is closer to Taiwan than to the main island of Okinawa, 450 kilometers (280 miles) to the northeast. Tokyo is 2,000 kilometers (1,243 miles) away. Given the geography, the islands have historically been so detached from Japan's major islands that some of the islanders here speak a local Ryukyuan language, with Japanese as their second tongue. Spend a few days here and you begin to wonder if you're still in Japan.

You easily could spend weeks slowly exploring the chain's various islands, but most visitors tend to focus on **Ishigaki-jima**, the second largest island in the group. At picturesque **Kabira Bay** on its northern shore, dense vegetation and turquoise waters sandwich thin strips of virgin white sand to create hypnotically beautiful views. The island's coastline also offers up numerous opportunities for snorkeling, diving and other water sports. From Ishigaki, boats run to **Taketomi-jima**, a great day-trip option just four kilometers southwest of Ishigaki, where

visitors can soak up traditional Okinawan culture like nowhere else in the Ryukyus (Okinawan islands). Thanks to strict building regulations, the villages here are still defined by sandy roads, traditional red-roofed housing and stone walls; modern trappings keep a very low profile. On its southern end, Taketomi also has some of the best beaches in the Yaeyamas.

If time isn't a concern, think about exploring farther afield. Boats run to the largest of the Yaeyamas, **Iriomote-jima** (30 kilometers; 18 miles) from Ishigaki, which is covered almost entirely in dense jungle and mangroves that provide the natural habitat for an incredible diversity of wildlife, including the critically endangered Iriomote Cat and a local variety of highly venomous pit viper. Not many foreign tourists make it out this far, but those who do take with them indelible subtropical memories.

Getting There Regular flights operate from Tokyo's Haneda Airport to Ishigaki, taking 3 hours 25 minutes, and also from Naha, taking 30 minutes. Boat services run from Ishigaki to and between the other islands in the chain. **Contact** Okinawa Convention & Visitors Bureau: ocvb.or.jp/en

From the thriving modern metropolis of Tokyo and the cultural heartland of Kyoto to the wilds of Hokkaido and Okinawa's pristine beaches, Japan has something spectacular to offer every traveler. This chapter will help you get the best out of Japan no matter how brief your stay, with suggestions for three great days in Tokyo, four more wonderful days exploring Kyoto and Nara, and plenty of other accessible day trips and memorable journeys. Get out there and experience as much of it as you can!

EXPLORING
TOKYO IN THREE DAYS
Discover the energetic metropolis's many faces

Tokyo, the "Eastern Capital," is relatively young by Japanese standards. When shogun Tokugawa Ieyasu chose the then fishing village of Edo as the site for his new base of power in 1603 and began construction of Edo Castle, imperial Kyoto had already been thriving for almost a thousand years. It wasn't until the Meiji Restoration of 1868 that the then flourishing Edo changed its name to Tokyo and became the country's official capital. Despite being almost totally destroyed twice since then (by the 1923 Great Kanto Earthquake and the bombing of World War II), Tokyo has blossomed into one of the world's foremost metropolises—an enthralling and at times dizzying blend of modern and unerringly traditional that is home to 35 million people living in a vast urban sprawl stretching almost unbroken from its center into the neighboring prefectures of Kanagawa, Chiba, Yamanashi and Saitama.

A Day in Northern Tokyo
Old neighborhoods and the latest gadgets

Tokyo's northeast is a fitting place to start exploring the city, as it is here in the neighborhoods of Ueno and Asakusa, and to a slightly lesser extent the electronics and *otaku* (geek) district of Akihabara, that Tokyo reveals more of its soul than anywhere else.

Akihabara: Electronics and Otaku

Electronics took off in Akihabara, two stations northeast of Tokyo Station, with the black market trading of radios and radio components immediately after World War II, and they continue to thrive in the area with a combination of megastores and hundreds of small-scale specialists. Akihabara's main street, **Chuo-dori**, and the side streets leading off of it teem with stores, from places like **Thanko** (thanko.jp), which specializes in quirky electronics such as odd-shaped USB devices and binoculars with built-in video recorders, to **Tsukumo Robot Kingdom** (robot.tsukumo.co.jp), where you can pick up all sorts of robots and robot parts. Then there are the megastores like **Laox**, **Ishimaru Denki** and, best of all, the giant **Yodobashi Akiba** (yodobashi-akiba.com), which opened on the east side of the station in 2005 and features six floors of home electronics covering everything from

Shopping in Akihabara

Senso-ji Temple in Asakusa

the latest cameras to cell phones to computers to even massage chairs.

Akiba's (to use the area's nickname) other face is far newer. Since the late 1990s the area has developed as a center for Japan's *otaku* (geek) subculture. Though they have a nerdy image, *otaku* have had a huge impact on Japan's economy and Akihabara is now positioned at the center of an *otaku* consumer market worth hundreds of billion yen annually. Wander through the comic stores, costume shops and video game stores that compete for space with the electronics on and around Chuo-dori and you'll see every *otaku* taste catered for. In particular, the large **Donkihote** (named after Don Quixote; donki.com) has an entire floor dedicated to *anime* (animation) and *manga* (comics) costumes, as well as being a good place to hunt for odd souvenirs, while on the opposite side of Chuo-dori **Gee Store Akiba** specializes solely in cosplay outfits and related goods. Another place from among many worth a shout out is the small **Tokyo Anime Center** (animecenter.jp) on the fourth floor of **Akihabara UDX Building**,

which has information on the latest happenings in Japanese animation and is home to a 3D theater, recording studio and numerous events.

Asakusa to Ueno

Moving further into Tokyo's northeast, to Ueno and Asakusa, takes you deep into *shitamachi* (literally "the low city"), one of the oldest and traditionally working class parts of the city. At Asakusa's heart is **Senso-ji** (see Japan's "Don't Miss" Sights, page 9), a magnificent temple complex that can trace its roots back almost 1,400 years. With the stalls that surround it and a steady flow of visitors, both tourists and locals, Senso-ji is lively all year round, but especially so in May with the **Sanja Matsuri** (page 112), a festival in honor of Senso-ji's founders that sees the streets of Asakusa taken over by a frenetic procession of portable shrines. Along with Tokyo's biggest fireworks display, the **Sumidagawa Hanabi Taikai** in July (page 113), and a **Samba Festival** (asakusa-samba.jp) in August, it's one of several times each year when Asakusa explodes into life.

Cherry blossom season at Ueno Park

A couple of blocks west of Senso-ji's towering five-story pagoda, Asakusa reveals the vestiges of its prewar days as Tokyo's premier entertainment district, with the tiny **Hanayashiki** (page 104), a delightfully retro amusement park that boasts Japan's oldest and perhaps most sedate roller coaster as well as many other simple vintage attractions that make it ideal for young children. Just southwest of there comes the northern end of **Rokku Broadway**, a street known for theaters like the **Engei Hall** (asakusaengei.com), which puts on a daily bill of slapstick comedy shows and traditional comic storytelling. Walk even further east and Asakusa's merchant roots are recalled along **Kappabashi-dori** (page 94), a street of 200 or so wholesale shops catering to the needs of Tokyo's restaurant industry and a great place to pick up an unusual souvenir or two.

Leaving Asakusa behind and heading a couple of stations away on the Ginza Line (or walking another 15 minutes east from Kappabashi-dori) brings you to **Ueno**, a part of town that like Asakusa has never strayed too far from its roots. The lively **Ameya Yokocho** street market here flourished on the back of black market goods as Tokyo rebuilt itself after World War II, although today the focus of the vocal touts and vendors is purely on legitimate goods.

Fish, vegetables, dried foods and teas, and low-price clothing and bags make up the bulk of the stores. Nearby, the sprawling **Ueno Park** contains, like Nikko (page 41), a **Tosho-gu shrine** and a five-story pagoda built in the 1600s for shogun Tokugawa Ieyasu. It's also home to several large lily-covered ponds, a small boating lake, Tokyo's biggest zoo, cherry blossom trees that bathe many of its walkways a delicate pink in spring, and some of the city's most interesting museums.

Ueno is most definitely museum country, with the **Shitamachi History Museum** (taitocity.net/taito/shitamachi), **Tokyo Metropolitan Art Museum** (tobikan.jp), **National Museum of Nature and Science** (kahaku.go.jp), **University Art Museum** (geidai.ac.jp/museum), **National Museum of Western Art** (nmwa.go.jp) designed by Le Corbusier and recently designated as a World Heritage Site), and **Tokyo National Museum** (tnm.jp). You could probably visit all in a long day, but if time is limited head first to Tokyo National Museum at the northern end of Ueno Park. With over 100,000 artifacts dating as far back as 3000 BC to the Jomon period, and taking in important works and exhibits from every major period in Japanese history thereafter, the National Museum has the biggest and best collection of Japanese

Monjayaki: A Taste of Old Tokyo

Two stations from Tsukiji (page 11) on the Oedo subway Line, **Tsukishima**, a man-made island reclaimed from Tokyo Bay in the 1890s, is a mix of expensive high-rise apartments and clusters of modest low-rise housing. Those contrasts, however, are not what singles Tsukishima out for special attention. Tsukishima's claim to fame in Japan is a dish peculiar to the Greater Tokyo area—*monjayaki*. Some people describe it in English as a kind of sticky pancake, but like so many Japanese foods it's difficult to find a simple translation that really does the dish justice. Born among the lower Edo-era classes as a way to make sure nothing went to waste, *monjayaki* comes to the table as a bowl of runny batter mixed with meat or seafood and a variety of finely cut vegetables. It's then fried on a hotplate built into the table until it takes on a consistency not too dissimilar to fried cheese, before you use little metal spatulas to scrape it up and eat directly from the hotplate. Perhaps because of Tsukishima's working-class roots—when it was known as a center for iron working—the low-cost food thrived in the area and today there are some 75 *monjayaki* restaurants on and around Tsukishima's aptly named "Monja Street." Just one bit of advice from someone who has suffered a burned tongue more than once—the metal spatula can get very hot!

history in the country. You will come out awed. On the other side of the park, the **Shitamachi History Museum** is dedicated specifically to local Tokyo history and is also highly recommended. On its ground floor is a reconstruction of a 1920s tenement row as well as a reconstructed merchant's house and other period reconstructions that provide an intriguing glimpse at prewar Ueno and Asakusa.

A Day in Western Tokyo
The city in all its modern guises

The west, in the neighboring Omotesando, Harajuku and Shibuya districts, is where Tokyo flexes its fashionable and youthful muscles. In Shinjuku, epitome of brash, modern Tokyo, the city shows off a little of everything: lights, energy, crowds and much more besides.

Shinjuku skyscrapers

Omotesando to Harajuku

Starting at Omotesando Station (on the Ginza and Hanzomon lines) and running almost one kilometer southeast to northwest, **Omotesando-dori** has been dubbed the Japanese Champs-Elysées and compared to Bond Street in London. Yet comparisons do the broad, zelkova-lined avenue no justice at all. Originally created as an approach to Meiji Jingu Shrine (page 33) in the Taisho era (1912–26), Omotesando-dori has become synonymous in recent years with two things: high-end shopping and modern architecture. The street is home to the flagship stores of such brands as Louis Vuitton, Prada and Dior as well as architectural gems like Tod's, a slim, L-shaped building designed by Toyo Ito that is encased in an enclosure of sharply angled concrete elements and polygonal glass plates. None of Omotesando's buildings, however, can compete with its centerpiece, **Omotesando Hills** (omotesandohills.com).

Designed by acclaimed architect Tadao Ando and opened in 2006, the 250-meter (820-foot)-long mall stretches along a quarter of Omotesando-dori's length. Some 100 shops and restaurants as well as 38 luxury apartments are housed on the inside, which is defined by a six-level atrium stretching three stories above

ground and three below, with a spiraling ramp connecting the different levels. Omotesando Hills is a modern architectural tour de force, but not one built without controversy. At its southeast end you'll find part of an old tenement building incorporated into the design, a nod from Ando to the charming, though near decrepit Dojunkai Aoyama Apartments that had been home to many a bohemian boutique and artisan over the years, but were torn down, amid much protest, to make room for Ando's ultramodern mall.

Directly opposite Omotesando Hills, and highlighting Tokyo's carefree approach to mixing and matching architecture, is the **Oriental Bazaar** (orientalbazaar. co.jp), a one-stop shop for almost every conceivable souvenir, from "I Love Tokyo" T-shirts to beautiful used kimono and fine antique furniture. On a street known for its cutting-edge architecture, you've got to applaud the brashness of the bazaar's faux oriental temple façade, which gives it the look of something transplanted straight from an ancient China-inspired theme park. Like the many other mismatched buildings in Tokyo, it poses the question of just who is in charge of planning permits.

At Omotesando's northwest end is **Harajuku Station** on the Yamanote Line, where high-end fashion abruptly gives way to more youthful tastes. Walk along Harajuku's narrow and perpetually heaving **Takeshita-dori** and it's all teen fashions, cosplay trends and brash, garish shop fronts. Even the art venues in the Harajuku area have a free-spirited, youthful air to them, in vibrant galleries like the freestyle **Design Festa Gallery** (page 107), where you are always guaranteed to find something dynamic and fresh on display. Not that the Harajuku area is only about youth culture. In the opposite direction to Takeshita-dori from Harajuku

Omotesando Hills

Shibuya Crossing

Station, **Meiji Jingu Shrine** and the adjoining **Meiji Jingu gardens** represent Tokyo at its greenest and most tranquil. Next to it, **Yoyogi Park** is the perfect place for a spot of people watching or a picnic, especially if you come on a weekend when it gets taken over by buskers, cosplayers and dancing rockabillies.

Shibuya to Shinjuku

Taking the JR Yamanote Line from Harajuku Station, within five minutes you can be in either **Shibuya** to the south or **Shinjuku** to the north. Though both are high energy, their stations teeming with commuters (**Shinjuku Station** is said to be the busiest in the world with an estimated three million

people passing through it daily) and their crowded streets awash with neon and noise, the vibe is distinctly different between the two areas. **Shibuya** serves almost as an extension of Harajuku, attracting teen and 20-something shoppers to places like the **109 Building** (page 93), the **Center Gai** shopping precinct (oddly, renamed Basketball Street in a 2011 marketing move that left people scratching their heads; everybody still calls it Center Gai) and **Seibu department store** (2.seibu.jp), while at night offering plenty of bars, clubs and restaurants for a younger crowd. **Shinjuku**, on the other hand, is a melting pot and no other part of the city really epitomizes modern Tokyo better. It is home to the

Iris Garden at Meiji Jingu Shrine

Tokyo Metropolitan Government (metro.tokyo.jp), whose Kenzo Tange-designed offices, with twin towers that reach 45 floors above Shinjuku's highrise west side, are one on Tokyo's most distinctive sights. Better yet, the twin towers have two free **observation decks** from where you can take in tremendous views of Mount Fuji to the west and sprawling cityscapes in all directionss.

Shinjuku is also known for its shopping, with the **Takashimaya**, **Marui** and **Isetan department stores** the most visible of numerous stores on the east and south sides of the station. Then there is **Shinjuku Gyoen**, a candidate for being Tokyo's finest garden (page 100). While in stark contrast to the peace and quiet of its park, Shinjuku also lays claim to Japan's most notorious red-light district, **Kabuki-cho**. In truth, while Kabuki-cho is the realm of many a sex club and *yakuza*-owned establishments, it also has plenty of great legitimate bars and restaurants that spill over into the neighboring area of **Shin Okubo** to the north (known as "Little Asia" because of its profusion of Korean and Southeast Asian

stores and restaurants) and directly east **Golden Gai**, a maze of narrow lanes crammed with tiny bars that have traditionally attracted a bohemian blend of artists, writers and other creatives. Also located here is the kitschy **Robot Restaurant** where a nightly performance of scantily clad ladies in robot costumes is like nothing you've ever seen.

A Day in Central Tokyo
Traditional meets contemporary

If the west end is Tokyo at its most chic, modern or youthful and the east best represents the city's more traditional elements, then it's central Tokyo where the two merge. **Tsukiji**, which attracts crowds with its high-energy wholesale market (see Japan's "Don't Miss" Sights, page 11), wouldn't feel out of place next to the bustling Ameya Yokocho in Ueno or alongside Kappabashi-dori. The biggest wholesale market in the world, in the region of 2,000 tons of seafood and other produce are sold daily here, but it's the early morning tuna auctions that are

Kabuki-cho entertainment district

the undoubted highlight—a high-octane blur of hand signals and yelling with which millions of yen's worth of prime tuna destined for the city's finest sushi restaurants changes hands.

Visit **Ginza**, a kilometer west of Tsukiji, and you get something entirely different—a wealthy yet more conservative Tokyo heavily influenced by classic Western tastes. Fittingly for a place whose name is derived from the silver mint Tokugawa Ieyasu established here in 1612 (though it later moved to nearby Nihombashi), Ginza has always been associated with wealth in one way or another. Most obviously, the area is home to prestigious department stores like **Mitsukoshi**, **Wako**, **Matsuya** and **Matsuzakaya** as well as numerous high-end European fashion retailers. It's here too that you'll find many of Tokyo's finest restaurants and exclusive bars and, of course, it's most expensive hostess clubs.

A short walk west of Ginza, the main attraction is the **Imperial Palace** (kunaicho.go.jp), or Kokyo. This is where the Emperor and imperial family live, and as such the palace and most of the 270-acre (109-hectare) grounds are off-limits. But that doesn't stop busloads of tourists visiting the outer gardens to get a glimpse of the palace's Fushimi Yagura tower protruding through dense woods, the stone double arches of Nijubashi Bridge dominating the foreground as it straddles the giant moat protecting the inner palace, before heading to the pleasant but by no means stunning **Imperial Palace East Gardens** (see page 100 for a list of the best gardens and parks in Tokyo).

Then there's **Roppongi**, a few kilometers southwest of the palace grounds, with its high-rise **Roppongi Hills** and **Tokyo Midtown** urban developments (see Japan's "Don't Miss" Sights, page 10), cosmopolitan nightlife and contemporary art venues like the **Mori Art Museum**

The Wako department store, Ginza

(page 106) and the **National Art Center** (page 106). If Roppongi was the only place you visited in Tokyo, you could be excused for coming away thinking the city is all glistening modern architecture and cool art and design.

Getting Around Tokyo has extensive and extremely reliable train and subway networks. The two subway systems, Tokyo Metro and Toei, both operate numerous lines, while the majority of trains are operated by Japan Railways (JR) and the rest by private rail companies such as Keio and Odakyu. Tickets for trains and subways are sold via vending machines situated near a station's ticket gates, with a signboard above the machine indicating the cost of a ticket to specific stations (sometimes in Japanese only). If you are not sure how much your fare will be, buy the cheapest ticket available (¥130–¥180, depending on the line) and then use a "fare adjustment machine" to pay the difference at your destinationn.

Anyone planning to use the train or subway often should consider buying an electronic **Pasmo** or **Suica pass** (¥500 deposit required), which can be precharged with multiples of ¥1,000 and then touched against scanners on the turnstiles upon entering and leaving a station to automatically deduct the fare. Pasmo (issued by Tokyo Metro) and Suica (issued by JR) can be used on any Toei, JR, Odakyu, Keio or Metro line. They can also be used on certain buses and even in convenience stores and on many vending machines. Tokyo's bus network is a nightmare to navigate and is best avoided, but taxis can be a handy option. They can be hailed on main streets in most urban areas or found at taxi ranks by most stations. Taxis are metered, with an initial rate of ¥660–¥740 that covers the first two kilometers and ¥80 for each subsequent 275 meters.

Although Tokyo has more than enough to keep visitors occupied, the areas immediately surrounding the metropolis offer their own array of not-to-be missed attractions, from a bustling Chinatown and an ancient seat of political and cultural power to Japan's most outrageously lavish shrine complex and the opportunity to soak in hot springs under the shadow of majestic Mount Fuji.

A Day in Kamakura
Japan's 13th-century capital

In 1192, **Kamakura**, only a tiny fishing village at the time, became the power base for Japan's first shogun, Yoritomo Minamoto. In the 140 years that followed, up until the Emperor Go Daigo brutally took power back to Kyoto in 1333, the town blossomed both as a cultural and political center, leaving behind a rich

Tsurugaoka Hachiman-gu shrine in Kamakura

legacy of temples and shrines that today make Kamakura a must stop on any visit to the Kanto region.

Although the sight most associated with Kamakura, the **Great Buddha** statue (Daibutsu), is actually located several stations away in the small coastal town of **Hase** (see Japan's "Don't Miss" Sights, page 12), Kamakura itself has much else to offer, not least some 85 historic temples and shrines. The greatest of those, the Zen temple of **Kencho-ji** (kenchoji. com), the head temple of the Rinzai sect of Buddhism and the country's oldest Zen training monastery, lies almost a kilometer north of Kamakura Station, surrounded by majestic cedar trees. None of the temple's buildings date back to the temple's foundation in 1253, when it was said to comprise an incredible 49 subtemples, yet the current (and still ancient) complex boasts a striking mix of Chinese and Japanese architectural styles that mark it out for attention.

Another 500 meters northwest of Kencho-ji, the Zen temple of **Engaku-ji** (engakuji.or.jp) has less historic importance than Kencho-ji but is more than a match architecturally, thanks to traditional Chinese Zen design elements and the towering cedars that enshroud the atmospheric complex. The temple is neighbored by another Kamakura highlight, **Tokei-ji** (tokeiji.com), a 13th-century nunnery turned temple, in earlier years known as a place of refuge for abused wives. Smaller and more peaceful than Kamakura's other sites, Tokei-ji is more than anywhere else in Kamakura a fine example of how traditional Japanese sensibilities are so entwined with an appreciation of nature. The temple grounds are decorated by apricot blossom in February, magnolia in March and irises in June before bush clover takes over in September.

Around Tokyo

Yokohama waterfront

Not that Kamakura is only about Zen. Shinto has left its mark too. On the way to Kencho-ji, at the end of the unusually broad Wakamiya-oji boulevard, which leads from Sagami Bay into the heart of Kamakura's temple district, the entrance to the majestic **Tsurugaoka Hachiman-gu Shrine** (hachimangu.or.jp) is marked by a towering, vermilion-lacquered *torii* gateway, beyond which a series of hump-back bridges lead visitors past two ponds that recall the violence of Kamakura's golden years. Designed by the wife of Yoritomo Minamoto, the shogun who made Kamakura the country's de facto capital in 1192, the four islands in the Heike pond are said to be symbolic of the death of Minamoto's enemies (the number four is associated with death in Japan), while the three islands in the Gempei pond signify the Chinese character for birth and, with it, Minamoto's victory.

Getting There Kamakura is served by Kamakura Station, which is best reached on the JR Yokosuka Line via Yokohama (about 30 minutes) or on the JR Shonan-Shinjuku Line from Shinjuku or Shibuya (about 1 hour). See Kanagawa Prefectural Tourism Association: kanagawa-kankou.or.jp

A Day in Yokohama
A historic and cosmopolitan port

The now-thriving port city of **Yokohama** was a fishing village with fewer than 100 houses when, in 1853, Commodore Matthew Perry of the US Navy sailed his "Black Ships" into Tokyo Bay in a move that paved the way for Japan to open its doors to foreign trade and exchanges. Where Tokyo, bordering Yokohama to the north, is modern and crowded, Yokohama, despite a population of 3.5 million, has a more spacious and in places more historic feel to it. And though Tokyo is the more cosmopolitan city, Yokohama undoubtedly wears its overseas connections with far more pride.

A major draw to Yokohama for Japanese is **Chinatown** (Chuka-gai), the most vibrant and biggest of Japan's three Chinatowns, which was established just 10 years after Perry first arrived on Japanese shores. The area's colorful, narrow streets hold nearly 200 restaurants and some 300 shops specializing in everything from Chinese groceries to dumpling steamers, attracting an estimated 18 million visitors annually. A few blocks north, and stretching several kilometers east to west, Yokohama's harbor front reveals remnants of the city's early development alongside its most modern attractions. From the pleasant **Yamashita-koen** (park) directly north of Chinatown, the waterfront unfolds eastward with the retired passenger liner, the *Hikawa-maru*, which prewar plied the water between Yokohama and Seattle but today is part of the worthwhile **NYK Maritime Museum** (nyk.com/rekishi). The waterfront then continues further east, passing through the large **Harbor View Park**, where British troops once had a garrison and which today retains several Western-influenced buildings that date to the late 1800s, and then reaches the 860-meter (1,500-foot)-long **Yokohama Bay Bridge**, which straddles Tokyo Bay, a beautiful sight when illuminated at night. South of the park and directly east of Chinatown, the chic **Motomachi** shopping district is defined by smart boutiques and cafes, quite different to its days as the zone where Japanese and foreigners would meet to trade in Yokohama's early years. Nearby, the **Gaijin Bochi** (Foreigner's Cemetery; yfgc-japan.com), a graveyard overlooking the bay that looks like it could have been transplanted from any old English village, is another reminder of Yokohama's past.

The first of several highlights west of Chinatown is **Shinko Island**, a man-made lump of land jutting out into the harbor and known for its giant 107.5-meter (353-foot)-high **Cosmo Clock 21 ferris wheel** and the **Akarenga** (yokohama-akarenga.jp), two beautifully renovated redbrick warehouses dating from 1911 that now form part of a chic waterfront entertainment, shopping and dining

complex. Beyond Shinko, Yokohama's otherwise fairly low-rise skyline shoots skyward with modern architectural aplomb in the fashionable **Minato Mirai** area. With the **Minato Mirai 21** (minatomirai21.com) waterside development at its heart, this area once occupied by warehouses and dockyards represents the most modern side of Yokohama, most notably with the imposing 296-meter (970-foot)-high **Landmark Tower** (yokohama-landmark.jp). If you fancy ending your day out in Yokohama with a drink, head to the Sky Café on Landmark Tower's 69th floor for its wonderful panoramic vista.

> **Getting There** Yokohama can be reached from Tokyo Station in 25 minutes on the Tokaido Line and from Shibuya Station in 25 minutes on the Tokyu Toyoko Line. See Yokohama Convention & Visitors Bureau: welcome.city.yokohama.jp/eng/travel

Hakone and Mount Fuji
See Japan's beloved mountain up close

With its natural hot springs, stunning mountain and lakeside scenery and proximity to **Mount Fuji** (see Japan's "Don't Miss" Sights, page 14), **Hakone** has long been a hugely popular destination for Tokyoites. Most come for

Sightseeing boats on Lake Ashi near Mount Fuji

Mount Fuji

either an attraction-packed day trip or a more relaxing overnight break that takes them through a well-worn but extremely worthwhile sightseeing route, beginning at Hakone-Yumoto Station with a ride on the charming, if not slightly rickety, **Hakone-Tozan switchback railway**. The two-carriage train winds its way upward through a succession of tiny stations before reaching the mountain village of **Gora**, on the way passing through Miyanoshita Station, home to the historic **Fujiya Hotel** (page 83), and Chokoku-no-Mori Station, which gives access to the excellent **Hakone Open Air Museum** (page 107).

From Gora, a funicular train whips travelers up to the 800-meter (2,625-foot) **Mount Soun** (Sounzan), from where another change of transportation sees them in a cable car being carried over Hakone's mountain ranges to the volcanic valley of **Owakudani** (owakudani. com), where the steam rising from sulfur vents and bubbling hot spring pools in the barren lunar valley creates a wonderfully eerie atmosphere. The hot springs here are used to cook Owakudani's

trademark *kuro-tamago,* boiled eggs blackened from cooking and which legend has it add seven years to the lives of anyone who eats one.

Moving away from the sulfur, the cable car eventually ends at **Lake Ashi** (Ashi-no-ko), where many travelers hop straight onto one of the mock galleons that cruise the lake. The real attraction here, however, when the Disneyesque pirate fleet is out of sight, are the views of Mount Fuji set beyond the lake's verdant rim, which itself is punctuated by the deep red giant *torii* gateway of **Hakone Shrine** (hakone-jinja.or.jp).

Getting There The Hakone area is served by Hakone-Yumoto Station, which can be reached on the Odakyu Line from Shinjuku Station in Tokyo in about 90 minutes. At ¥5,640, the Hakone Free Pass is a great way to cut costs traveling to and in the Hakone area. The pass is issued by Odakyu Railways and covers the train fare to and from Hakone from Shinjuku as well as three days of unlimited use of the Hakone-Tozan line, the Hakone Cable Car and the Hakone Cruise Boat on Lake Ashi. It also gives discounts at an extensive list of museums, restaurants and shops in the area. For details: odakyu.jp/english/deels/freepass/hakone See Hakone Tourist Information: hakone.or.jp

A Day in Nikko
Magnificent shrines and scenery

For many, **Nikko** has come to mean the elaborately decorated buildings that make up Tokugawa Ieyasu's **Tosho-gu Shrine** complex (page 13), a collection of World Heritage temples and shrines surrounded by ancient cryptomeria forests. As one of Japan's most visited historic destinations, it's understandable that Tosho-gu dominates Nikko's tourist brochures, yet there's far more to Nikko, by landmass the country's third largest city, than Ieyasu's shrine.

Before visiting Tosho-gu, the first site of interest for anyone coming via bus from Tobu Nikko Station is the oft photographed **Shinkyo Bashi** (get off at the Shinkyo bus stop), a striking vermilion bridge that was built for the exclusive use of *daimyo* and their entourages en route to Tosho-gu. From there, the entourage walked to what is now the first stop for many Nikko visitors, **Rinno-ji**, a temple complex of the Tendai sect. Rinno-ji's main hall, the Sanbutsudo, is covered for renovation work until 2021, but as the hall's name suggests ("Three Buddha Hall"), it's the three giant gilded Buddha and Kannon statues inside, not the building itself, that make Rinno-ji a must visit.

After **Tosho-gu** (covered in detail on page 13), if you have still have the energy for one more religious site, then proceed to **Futarasan Shrine** (shinkyo.net), a short walk west. Far easier on the eye than Tosho-gu with its understated design, the shrine is a calming place to take a break, either sipping *matcha* green tea at its traditional teahouse or strolling through its peaceful garden.

Nikko has other attractions further afield too. A 45-minute bus ride from Tosho-gu, and easily incorporated into a Nikko day trip from Tokyo if you make an early start, **Lake Chuzenji** at the base of the volcanic **Mount Nantei** is a lovely spot for boating, fishing and lakeside walks, especially in autumn when the dense mountain woods surrounding the lake turn an earthy palette of reds and yellows. The real draw to Chuzenji, however, are the **Kegon Falls**, arguably the most famed waterfalls in Japan, which cascade spectacularly 97 meters (318 feet) down a lush, rugged gorge situated just a few hundred meters east of the lake.

Getting There Tobu Nikko Station can be reached on the Tobu Line from Asakusa in Tokyo in about 2 hours. From Tobu Nikko Station, buses make the short run to Tosho-gu and on to Chuzenji frequently. See Nikko Tourist Association: nikko-jp.org.

Kegon Falls and Lake Chuzenji in Nikko

EXPLORING KANAZAWA AND THE JAPAN ALPS
Excursions to the west of Tokyo

When was the last time you had solid gold flakes sprinkled on glistening fish roe sushi or bit into a luscious cream puff dusted with gold powder? This bit of luxury is assured to visitors to Kanazawa, along with many other attractions that are well worth a visit to Honshu's western shore. The new Shinkansen bullet train line from Tokyo makes this an easy weekend excursion from the city. The Tourist Information counter inside the sparkling new station is superb and offers excellent maps and advice.

A Day in Kanazawa
Renowned gardens in the "City of Crafts"

Convenient bus services start at the east and west gates of the station bringing visitors to the major sights. Walking to Kanazawa Castle and Kenroku-en Garden are good options, too, taking perhaps 40 minutes. To reach more sights, however, the all-day ¥500 Kanazawa Loop Bus (departing every 15 minutes) covers the Higashi Chaya Geisha District, Kenroku-en, Castle Park, the 21st Century Museum of Contemporary Art, the Naga-machi Buke-yashiki (Samurai homes) district and the Omi-cho food market. There is also a Kenroku-en shuttle that goes directly to the garden and from there visitors can explore the area at their own pace.

Try to arrive in Kanazawa before noon, and head straight to the vibrant **Omi-cho market** (get off at Omi-cho Ichiba-kan) brimming with seafood products. There are plenty of counter-only restaurants and one of Japan's most renowned sushi shops on the ground floor. Tickets are issued to customers outside the shop but waiting times are likely to be long on weekends and in high season. If pressed for time, try the other restaurants on the second floor. Those who are not so fond of raw fish can ask for *tendon*, bowls of rice topped with crispy tempura. Vegetarians can ask for vegetables only. All appetites and tastes are accommodated.

Omi-cho market

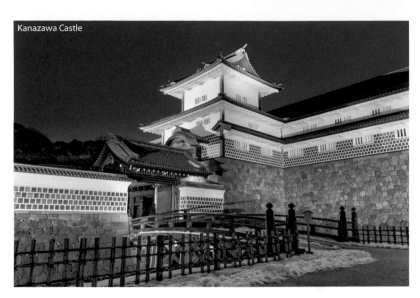

Kanazawa Castle

The vast **Kanazawa Castle** grounds, which are open from dawn to dusk, hint at the size of this once magnificent structure that was lost to fires and an earthquake over the centuries. From 2000, a reconstruction faithful to the ancient technique of joinery was undertaken. Inside, drop-down video screens show the mastery required to build a medieval castle. To one side of the screens is a small-scale model of the castle that allows visitors a detailed look at the interior beams and pillars.

From the bus stop, walk across the bridge that spans the road into the castle grounds. The main group of buildings is straight ahead. (A newly renovated castle keep to the right may also be entered.) After passing through the massive wood and iron Hashizumen-mon Gate, pause for a second to absorb the immensity of the structure.

Arrows guide visitors through the interior of the building and up and down steep stairways. Visitors are provided with plastic bags to carry their shoes while inside the castle.

Exiting the castle, visitors can either stroll through the park-like castle grounds or enter the **Kenroku-en Garden** via the main ticket booth back down the slope and across the bridge (combination tickets for both the castle and Kenroku-en cost ¥500; free for seniors over 70). Definitely try the gold flake-sprinkled soft ice cream cone for ¥500 or one completely coated in gold for ¥1,000 at the shops here. It tastes

Kenroku-en Garden

as fabulous as it looks and you will definitely want to join others who are holding up their gorgeous treats for selfies.

Garden paths wind through plantings of seasonal flowers past ponds, stepping-stones, stone lanterns and picturesque tableaus as well as the old residence of Lord Maeda (¥400 admission). During the winter months, unique straw-rope bindings on the trees and bushes (*yuki-zuri*) are a special attraction for visitors. Each branch is secured and tied to a central pole and knotted at the top, sort of a winter "Maypole" (see photo on page 16).

Strolling the garden can easily take an hour or two, but visitors should also visit the **Museum of Traditional Arts and Crafts** (Ishikawa-densankan.jp) at the Kodatsuna entrance. The shop here features crafted items—hand-painted candles, glass items or textiles—that many visitors find irresistible The second floor has an excellent display of products from this "City of Crafts."

Visitors can also walk to the Mayumi-zaka entrance of the garden and cross the street to visit the ultramodern **21st Century Museum of Contemporary Art**. Admission fees depend on the current exhibit but the circular glass structure is free to enter. (Closed Mondays, as are most Japanese museums.)

Take the loop bus to the **Naga-machi samurai homes district** where warriors faithful to Lord Maeda resided. The gardens of the private homes in this district are unlike the Zen gardens of Kyoto, which have an open plot of land covered with combed sand and stones or the older vast stroll gardens with intersecting paths. The homes in this part of Japan condense a vast amount of scenery into a very small and contained space, the most famous of which is the **Nomura house and garden**, which can be viewed from the first and second stories. Varying heights and layering of greenery enclose this compact garden that displays amazing horticultural and design skills.

The Kaga Hot Springs
Onsen towns just south of Kanazawa

An hour-long train ride south of Kanazawa reveals more wonders. The Hokuriku area has several of Japan's finest spa towns, collectively known as

Nomura house and garden in the Naga-machi district

Hokuriku Onsen. Recommended is **Yamashiro Onsen**, since it is also home to the ancient Kutaniyaki Exhibition Hall and the 1,300-year-old Natadera Temple. To get there, take the JR Raicho (Thunderbird) express from Kanazawa Station to Kaga (40 minutes), then a taxi or the Can bus. Tickets for the bus (one day ¥1,000; 2 day ¥1,200; children ¥500) can be purchased at the Kaga Tourist Information counter in Kaga Station. Also ask for a map of the town and Yamashiro Onsen. The Can bus also goes to three other hot spring towns and Natadera Temple.

In the town center of Yamashiro are the charming two-story **Soyu** and **Ko-Soyu bathhouses**, which were recently rebuilt. After a refreshing soak, bathers can retreat to the second floor for something to drink and chat with other visitors. A building across the plaza serves simple meals. To the left of **Hotel Yamashitaya** is a place to sit and soak tired feet. (Bring a small towel.)

Just a few minutes' walk from the bathhouses, an impressive sculpted stone and moss garden forms the approach to the **Iroha house and workshop** of famed potter and gourmet Kitaoji Rosanjin (1883–1959), who was a largely self-taught ceramist, calligrapher and writer. His workshop and study, with its high exposed dark wooden beams and small attached display room, offer a glimpse of

Kanazawa Area

A foot bath at Yamashiro Onsen

the artist's influential life. A cup of tea is offered to visitors. (Open 9 a.m. to 5 p.m., closed Wednesday; admission ¥500.)

One of the specialties of Yamashiro is the highly decorated Kutaniyaki pottery, which is displayed in the **Kutaniyaki Exhibition Hall**, a 10-minute walk from the Rosanjin house. The house features the present kiln, still used for firing. It was built in 1940 and is the oldest Kutani ware kiln in existence. Within the building on this site is a studio with rooms divided according to all the processes involved in producing Kutaniyaki ware. Two of the ancient climbing kilns are on view. (Open 9 a.m. to 5 p.m., closed Tuesday; admission ¥310.)

The **Kutaniyaki Art Museum** is a few minutes walk from nearby Daishoji Station. Besides the fine exhibits on display, there are many shops in the vicinity for visitors to procure a memento of the luscious-colored ceramics (open 9 a.m. to 5 p.m., closed Monday; admission ¥500). Another worthwhile sight is **Natadera Temple**, a 20-minute ride on the Can bus. This Shingon sect Buddhist temple is well known for its dense greenery, rocky outcroppings with Buddhist images and pathways, and is especially beautiful in the autumn (admission ¥600).

The Important Cultural Heritage village of Shirakawa-go

A Visit to Shirakawa-go
Fascinating World Heritage villages

Three villages in the Gokoyama area—Ainokura, Suganuma and Shirakawa-go—have all been designated Important Cultural Heritage Sites. Of these, the best known is **Shirakawa-go**, which was established in the 11th century.

Being remote and isolated, residents here had to grow everything needed to survive the long and severe winters, supplementing their income by cultivating silk worms fed on the leaves of mulberry bushes planted in the narrow valley. The silk cocoons were kept in the warm upper stories of the thatched houses until ready to be spun into threads.

Several of the houses are now open to the public. The **Iwase Family Residence** and **Gokayama Minzoku-kan Folklore Museum** (admission ¥300) both date back 300 years. Some houses offer overnight stays although you need to book in advance and be aware that the amenities are basic. The Tourist Information Center in Kanazawa Station is very helpful.

The easiest way to get to Shirakawa-go is to take a train to Takayama and a bus to the village. Another way (weather permitting) is to take the Nohi Highway bus from Kanazawa Station. The journey takes about an hour, traversing some breathtaking mountain scenery.

Further into the Japan Alps

From Shirakawa-go, travelers can venture on to the mountain town of **Hida-Takayama** via the Nohi bus, a 2 hr. 20 min. ride or via Takayama JR Station. Hida-Takayama is nestled deep in the Japan Alps. Severe winters, poor soils and dense forests restricted its residents' agricultural activities but were a boon to developing superb carpentry skills. The local homes and inns are constructed of massive timbers, blackened by hundreds of years of candles and cooking fires.

One especially fine example is the **Yoshishima Heritage House**, with its dark, high interlocking beams, massive rooms and sunken hearths. It is a trip back to the 17th-century lifestyle of a successful merchant.

The **Kusakabe Folk Craft Museum** is another architectural gem constructed of ancient timbers with rooms displaying the artistic culture that developed here, which is still valued by its residents.

From Takayama JR Station, trains travel south to Nagoya where connections to Tokyo, Kyoto and Osaka are easy to make.

Nishiki-koji Market

A thousand years as the nation's cultural and political center, until Tokyo officially assumed the role with the Meiji Restoration in 1868, have left Kyoto with a rich cultural and historical legacy that few other cities can even dream of matching. Kyoto's 2,000 exquisite temples and shrines are the most obvious remnants of the city's halcyon days, but add to that its world-renowned *kyo-ryori* cuisine, its 17 UNESCO World Heritage Sites, a collection of fine museums and galleries, Japan's most famous geisha district, and much, much more, and Kyoto is simply unmissable

A Day in Central Kyoto
Delightful shopping and a mighty castle

First impressions of Kyoto can catch visitors off-guard. The ultramodern glass and steel design of **Kyoto Station**, through which the majority of travelers arrive, is a far cry from the tourist brochure images of geisha and cherry blossom-accented temples. Move northward from the station, into the center of Kyoto, and **Shijo-dori** street could have been transplanted straight from Tokyo. Alongside the **Daimaru** and **Takashimaya** department stores are familiar coffee shop chains and brand name boutiques like Luis Vuitton, Swarovski and Jill Stuart. Second impressions, however, are far better. Third impressions

will have you hooked. Even amid all of Kyoto's modern trappings, you never need to look very far for reminders of Kyoto's glorious past.

Running parallel to Shijo-dori, a block to the north, **Nishiki-koji Market** has been Kyoto's main food market since the 17th century and it still affords a look at the more traditional side of the city. The covered market is a riot of color and aromas that stretches for several blocks along a single narrow street, offering ample opportunities to stop and sample delicacies, from Kyoto's numerous tofu variations and pickles to dried fish, handmade noodles, sweets and all sorts of other local fare.

Entrance to Nijo Castle

Heading a little northwest of Nishiki and Shijo, the imposing **Nijo Castle** (city.kyoto.jp/bunshi/nijojo) looms into sight. With grounds spreading over 275,000 square meters (329,000 square yards), this World Heritage Site was originally built by Tokugawa Ieyasu in the early 1600s and expanded by subsequent generations. The current structure comprises two concentric rings of fortifications, gardens and several palaces. With the Tokugawa shogunate lasting as long as it did unchallenged, the castle's defenses were never put to the test in anger, but looking at the giant stone walls you would imagine they would have withstood any feudal onslaught. And should someone have planned a more subtle attack, the castle was designed to withstand subterfuge too, the "nightingale" floors in the **Ninomaru Palace** (a must see for its intricately decorated screen doors) squeaking like birds should an intruder try to enter by stealth.

A Day in Eastern Kyoto
Ancient temples, geisha and art

As Shijo-dori reaches its eastern end, crossing the **Kamo-gawa River** and leaving the city center behind, it leads into some of Kyoto's most historic sites. If one had to pick a single eastern standout, it would have to be **Kiyomizu-dera** (see Japan's "Don't Miss" Sights, page 18), a temple complex set against a rich natural backdrop that changes hues with each season, from the pink of cherry blossoms in spring to lush greens in summer, through to earthy reds in autumn and the occasional dabble of white in winter, although there are other attractions that push Kiyomizu close.

Gion, just south of Shijo's eastern end, isn't the only place in Kyoto where you will find geisha (properly called *geiko* in Kyoto), but it is the most famous. The back streets here, lined with wooden

Chado: The Way of Tea

The tea ceremony has long held an important position in traditional Japanese culture. Known as either *chado* or *sado* in Japanese, the Zen-influenced ritual is performed with both calm precision and grace, turning the otherwise simple process of mixing powdered green tea (*matcha*) and hot water into one of Japan's finer forms of artistic expression. If you would like to experience the ceremony, then Kyoto is the place to do it. Try either the small *tatami*-floored **En Teahouse** in **Gion** (teaceremonyen.com), which does four short ceremonies for groups daily in English for ¥2,500 per person, or **Ran Hotei** (ranhotei.com), a teahouse set in an old renovated townhouse where a 90-minute tea ceremony lesson with Canadian tea master Randy costs ¥3,500.

At **Tea Shop Kouroan**, one can learn about the process of growing and making powdered green tea (*matcha*) and leaf tea (*sencha*). The hour-long explanation is accompanied by both types of tea and costs ¥1,800. A private tea lesson is ¥3,700 (kouroan.com/).

Geiko in the Gion district

townhouses and teahouses are lit with outside lanterns that provide the perfect backdrop should you catch a fleeting glimpse of the area's geisha as they flit between appointments. Save for the occasional busload of tourists that drop by and stalk the geisha for photo ops, Gion usually exudes a remarkably calm vibe given it's in the heart of the city. In July, the area also hosts the **Gion Matsuri** (see Festivals and Events, page 111), a festival defined by its procession of floats, traditional music and jam-packed crowds (more than a million people attend each year). The Gion Matsuri kicks off at **Yasaka Shrine**, which was first built in the late 7th century and now marks the end of Shijo-dori with its vivid orange and white two-tiered gateway. The shrine is equally colorful in spring when the adjoining **Maruyama Park** bursts into a frenzy of pink as the annual cherry blossom front sweeps northward across the country. If you are lucky enough to be in Kyoto in late March or early April, it's one of the prettiest places to take a packed lunch and picnic under Japan's favorite petals.

A 20-minute bus ride northeast of Yasaka leads to the magnificent **Ginkaku-ji** (shokoku-ji.or.jp). Known as the Silver Pavilion, this World Heritage temple doesn't actually have an ounce of silver on it. Legend has it that, when built

in the 1480s to be a retirement home for the then shogun, it was due to be covered in silver leaf. The project, however, ran out of money and Ginkaku-ji remained un-gilded. Looking at the now Zen temple, the lack of silver is no loss at all. In fact, while **Kinkaku-ji** (page 17) awes with the grandiose design and gilding of its main building, it is Ginkaku-ji's understated beauty that better represents Japan's fine artistic sensibilities, with its calculated combination of subtle components: a simple yet enigmatic raked sand garden, perfectly sculpted trees, a pond positioned to catch rippled reflections of the main building, and a vantage point on a wooded hillside from where you can take it all in.

In the eastern part of the city, Kyoto also takes an arty turn. Ideal for when it's raining or if Kyoto's summer heat and humidity become too much, there are three great museums in the area: the **National Museum of Modern Art** (momak.go.jp), where the focus is on local artists predominantly from the 20th century; the **Hosomi Museum** (emuseum. or.jp), which along with its collection of Asuka to Edo-era artifacts incorporates traditional and modern design elements that stretch as far as *sukiya*-style tearooms; and the **Kyoto Municipal Museum of Art** (city.kyoto.jp/bunshi/kmma), which houses a renowned collection of post Meiji-era fine art.

The reflection pond at Ginkaku-ji

A Day in Western Kyoto
Zen gardens and a little kitsch

While Kyoto's east side is crammed with historical sites, the attractions are spread more thinly on the western side of the city. What the west boasts, however, is quality over quantity. The west side's most prominent site, the majestic gilded temple of **Kinkaku-ji** (see Japan's "Don't Miss" Sights, page 17) is understandably one of Japan's most heralded attractions. Nearby is another, albeit far more understated temple, **Ryoan-ji** (ryoanji.jp).

The *karesansui* (dry landscape) garden at Ryoan-ji is one of Japan's most captivating mysteries. Despite centuries of theorizing and study, there is still no consensus on who designed the garden, when it was created or what the design means. For some, the garden's 15 rocks, some accented with a vibrant green moss that contrasts with the 30 meter (100 feet) by 10 meter (33 feet) rectangular patch of off-white gravel on which they are arranged, represent small islands on an ocean. Some look upward for inspiration and suggest the rocks depict clouds, the gravel sky. Still others believe the cryptic communion of rock clusters and gravel represents a tiger carrying a cub across a river or forms a map of Chinese Zen monasteries. And the curiosities don't end there. Try and find a vantage point from which to view all 15 rocks at once and you can only fail. From any given spot, you will never be able to count more than 14 unless you have reached spiritual enlightenment through meditation.

Back to the mystery of the garden's age, most likely the garden was created when Ryoan-ji became a temple shortly after the Onin War of 1467–77, a period during which much of Kyoto, including the estate that formerly occupied Ryoan-ji's land, was destroyed. As for Ryoan-ji's creator, that is less clear. It is believed the renowned 15th-century artist and landscape gardener Soami had some hand in the design and construction of the garden, but with different craftsmen's names carved on the back of some of the rocks and a lack of temple records, we will probably never know. Not that it really matters. As with the riddle of

Kyo-ryori: The Finest Kyoto Cuisine

In a nation that justifiably prides itself on the variety and quality of its cuisine, *kyo-ryori* sits at the head of the epicurean table. Although there are variations of *Kyo-ryori* (*yusoku-ryori* eaten by the Emperor and nobility; *kaiseki-ryori* featuring a multitude of small dishes; *shojin-ryori* vegetarian cuisine eaten by monks and priests; and the more casual *obanzai* style of home cooking), each style exploits the natural flavors of seasonal produce, each is presented exquisitely and within a seasonal context, and each is delicately cooked. For places to try *kyo-ryori* at its very best, see the restaurant listings on page 87.

The Zen rock garden at Ryoan-ji

Ryoan-ji's design, the answer is probably not what counts but the contemplation that leads to it.

Daitoku-ji, a Zen temple complex to the east of Kinkaku-ji, is another of the west side's Zen highlights. Although founded in 1315 and constructed with funding from the emperors Hanazono and Go-Daigo, like so many places in Kyoto Daitoku-ji had to be rebuilt after being burned down during the Onin War. Home to numerous cultural treasures as well as the resting place of warlord Oda Nobunaga, the grounds of the rebuilt main temple also represent a study in classical Zen layout, featuring a tall, two-bayed gateway, a Buddha hall, a Dharma hall, an abbot's quarters and bathhouse, and a sutra library, a blueprint echoed in so many Japanese Zen temples. Of the 22 subtemples associated with Daitoku-ji, two are well worth visiting for their gardens: **Daisen-in** for its famed stone garden that uses pebbles and rocks to depict a Chinese landscape painting, and **Ryogen-in** for its four small *karesansui*.

Finally, south of Ryoan-ji, **Koryu-ji** (also called Uzamasa-dera) is believed to be the oldest temple in Kyoto. Established in 603, though the current buildings don't date that far back, the temple houses many exquisite and ancient statues, including the Buddhist statue of Miroku Bosatsu (Future Buddha), a carving of a slender figure sitting in deep thought, said to have been given to Prince Shotoku (the man thought to have established Koryu-ji and who founded Horyu-ji in Nara, page 19) by the Korean court in the 7th century.

If you are feeling templed out (and Kyoto can definitely do that to you), you could do far worse than recharge with some classic Japanese kitsch at **Kyoto Toei Studio Park** (or Eigamura; toei-eigamura.com). This theme park-cum-TV and movie set is designed to resemble an Edo-era town, through which visitors can stroll dressed in period costumes while perusing exhibits on the numerous TV shows and movies made here, exploring the tricks and traps of a *ninja* house and other mock buildings, and best of all taking in live theatrical performances that include *ninja* shows and wonderfully overacted *samurai* battles.

Southern Kyoto and Nara

The birthplace of Japanese civilization

A trip out of Kyoto to the ancient capital of Nara, stopping en route to take in several historic attractions in southern Kyoto, makes for a long yet extremely rewarding day out.

The day could begin one station south of Kyoto Station, at Tofukuji Station on the Nara Line, with **Tofuku-ji Temple** (tofu-kuji.jp). Given that Tofuku-ji is home to a famous 15th-century Zen-style gate, Japan's oldest, as well as a collection of beautifully designed gardens, it's amazing that the complex rarely attracts huge crowds. In fact, you can usually explore some of its 23 subtemples in a peace and quiet unimaginable at Ryoan-ji or Kinkaku-ji. To be nigh on alone when visiting 20th-century garden designer Mirei Shigemori's contemporary take on traditional Zen gardens, which surround Tofukuji's main hall (the Hojo), is a simply delightful way to start a day.

From Tofukuji Station, one stop farther south on the Nara Line (although you can also walk quite easily from Tofuku-ji), is

Fushimi Inari Shrine

Fushimi Station and the wonderful **Fushimi Inari Taisha** (inari.jp). Dating to the early 700s, the shrine is known for its 10,000 vermilion *torii* gateways, which cover 4 kilometers (2.5 miles) of winding pathways leading up and around wooded mountains, creating one of Kyoto's most distinctive sights and most mesmerizing walks. Even further south on the Nara Line, about 30 minutes from Kyoto Station, comes **Uji**, a town in part known for its tea fields and the highly valued leaves they produce, in part for being the site of one of the country's most recognizable temples, **Byodo-in** (byodoin.or.jp), the temple depicted on the back of the ¥10 coin. Like many temples in and around Kyoto, Byodo-in began life as an aristocratic villa, one of many that made Uji something of an aristocrat's retreat in the early days of Kyoto's time as capital. In the 11th century, the villa was converted into a temple and a great hall (the Phoenix Hall) was added to house a gilded statue of Amida that remains in situ today in the original hall, whose structure stretches out left and right like a heron extending its wings in flight, about to land on the glistening pond before it.

Leaving Byodo-in behind, and continuing south on the Nara Line, comes **Nara**. Situated just 35 kilometers (19 miles) south of Kyoto, the ancient city tends to be overshadowed by its illustrious neighbor. But it hasn't always been like that. Before Kyoto became Japan's capital in 794, it was Nara, considered by Japanese scholars to be the birthplace of Japanese civilization, which served as Japan's seat of power and culture through most of the 8th century. More than a thousand years later, in 1993, the city pipped Kyoto to another honor: Nara's **Horyu-ji Temple** (see Japan's "Don't Miss" Sights, page 19) became the first site in Japan to receive World Heritage status.

Competing with Horyu-ji as Nara's star attraction is **Todai-ji Temple** (todaiji. or.jp), a World Heritage Site originally founded in 745 by the Emperor Shomu at a cost so great it is said the Imperial court nearly went bankrupt during the 15 years it took to complete the temple and its network of subtemples. It's not hard to see why. Beyond the towering Nandai-mon gateway to the great temple complex stands one of the largest wooden buildings in the world, the 57-meter (187-foot)-long, 50-meter (164-foot)-wide Daibutsu-en, which was built to house a 15-meter (49-foot)-tall bronze statue of Buddha, Japan's largest bronze image. Unlike his Great Buddha (Daibutsu) cousin in Kamakura (page 12), the 500-ton bronze Daibutsu of Nara has had a much harsher life since it was unveiled in 752. The partially remodeled statue had its head lopped off in a 9th-century

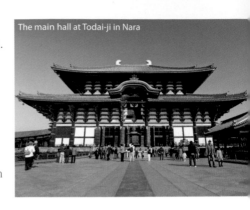
The main hall at Todai-ji in Nara

earthquake, his hands melted twice in fires in the 12th and 16th centuries, and his gilding has blackened with age.

Making up Nara's star trio of temples is the 7th-century **Kofuku-ji Temple** (kofukuji.com) and its 600-year-old five-story pagoda, the original of which was moved here from Kyoto in the early 8th century. Anyone with an interest in traditional Asian artwork will be fascinated by the treasures Kofuki-ji has been entrusted with. The 15th-century Token-do hall just north of Kofuku-ji's pagoda houses a breathtaking collection of Buddhist statues that date as far back as the 8th century, while the modern Kokuhokan Hall is home to Nara's most famed image, a standing statue of the three-headed, six-armed Ashura, one of Buddha's guardians. Its craftsmanship is simply exquisite.

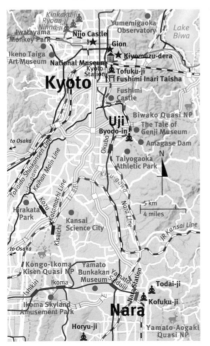

Getting There Tokyo's buses are a nightmare but Kyoto's are a godsend. Not only are almost all of Kyoto's main sights covered by the city's extensive bus network but the buses are great value for money and easy to navigate. Pick up a ¥600 day pass for the buses and an English-language copy of the Kyoto bus network map from Tourist Information in Kyoto Station or the ticket office at the bus terminal on Kyoto Station's north side, or a ¥900 bus-and-subway all-day ticket. The Karasuma subway line runs north–south and passes through Kyoto and Shijo stations while the Tozai subway line runs east–west through the city center. Kyoto's several JR lines and the private commuter lines of Keihan and Hankyu offer alternative transport.

EXPLORING
OSAKA AND KANSAI
The Kansai region is home to Japan's second city, feudal legacies and much more

Known among Japanese for its distinctive local dialect known as Osaka-ben, gregarious locals (some Tokyoites might just say loud!) and lively nightlife, Osaka is a refreshing change of pace from the temples and shrines of Kyoto 40 kilometers (25 miles) to the west.

A Day in Osaka
Japan's bustling second city

There's no better place to get your bearings in Osaka than at the city's most prominent feature, the eight-story **Osaka Castle** (osakacastle.net). Originally built by Toyotomi Hideyoshi

in 1585 and destroyed and rebuilt more than once since then, the current structure dates only to 1931, but that doesn't make it any less impressive as it dominates the skyline from its hilltop perch in the center of the city. From the upper floors you can take in sweeping city views of the surrounding land, which are almost as impressive as the several floors of fine feudal artifacts and other historic exhibits within the castle

Southwest of the castle is **Dotombori** (served by Namba Station), Osaka's main entertainment district, an area that after nightfall pulsates with energy and has no shortage of great restaurants and bars (see page 92 for recommendations). In the same area, a little to the east, is **Den Den Town**, Osaka's answer to Akihabara, the **National Theater** (ntj.jac.go.jp), where you can take in *bunraku* puppet plays, and **Shitenno-ji Temple** (shitennoji. or.jp). Although mostly a modern rebuild, Shitenno-ji's stone *torii* gateway, unusual in a temple, dates to the 1200s. The temple itself was founded in 593 by Prince Shotoku, who was also behind the ancient

Dotombori, Osaka's entertainment district

Osaka Eats: The Joys of Okonomiyaki

The Japanese have a wonderful way of associating every place with a particular food. In Osaka's case, they are spoiled for choice. First and foremost there's *okonomiyaki*, a mix of shredded cabbage and batter that's augmented with meat or seafood and fried

into a kind of pancake that's then slavered with thick brown sauce, sprinkled with dried seaweed and dried bonito flakes and ideally washed down with a good chilled lager. Pushing *okonomiyaki* close as the city's most known dish is *takoyaki*, chunks of octopus fried into battered balls that then get covered with the same thick sauce and toppings as *okonomiyaki*.

temples of Nara (page 19), making it the oldest temple in the country. Directly north of Dotombori is the shopping area of **America-mura** (literally America Village), which gets its name from once being the place to pick up cheap US fashions but is now full of boutiques catering to teens and 20 somethings.

In the north of the city, heading west from the castle, the attractions include the **Museum of Oriental Ceramics** (moco.or.jp) and its magnificent collection of over 1,000 Japanese, Korean and Chinese ceramic pieces, as well as **Tenmangu**, a 10th-century shrine dedicated to Sugawara no Michizane, Japan's patron saint of scholars. Visit on the 5th, 10th or 25th of any month and you'll see students visiting the shrine to pray for academic success. Come on July 24th or 25th and you'll get a far livelier welcome as the shrine's annual festival reaches fever pitch with fireworks, a procession of floats and lantern-lit boats plying the nearby canal.

Out of the center of the city, by the western waterfront, is where Osaka gets family friendly with **Universal Studios Japan** (page 105), a 140-acre (16-hectare) site featuring copies of the most popular rides at its sister parks in the US, along with some Japan-only attractions such as a daily Hello Kitty parade (ideal if you have young kids into things pink and sparkly!). Rounding off a family day out in the area is the massive **Osaka Aquarium** (page 105), the biggest aquarium in the world.

A Day in Kobe
European architecture, Chinatown and modern amusements

For many outside Japan, **Kobe** is known for the disaster that befell the port city on January 17th, 1995. In the early hours of that morning, a magnitude 7.3 earthquake struck just 20 kilometers (12 miles) from the city center, claiming 6,433 lives and causing damage in excess of $100 billion. Kobe's recovery hasn't yet seen it reclaim its pre-quake status as Japan's leading shipping port, but in all other respects the city has undoubtedly bounced back to life.

Kobe's Kitano-cho district

Most travelers reach Kobe, 30 kilo-meters (19 miles) to the east of Osaka, via the trunk railway that stops at Shin-Kobe Station. From here it's only a few blocks west before they are in the thick of Kobe's most popular sightseeing action,

the old **Kitano-cho** district with its blend of old European and US architecture harking back to the foreign traders who began living here after Kobe opened itself to overseas trade in 1868. Although the old brick buildings are pleasant

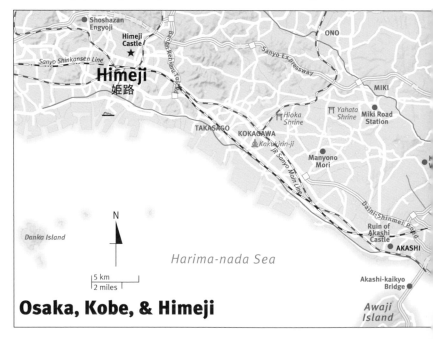

Osaka, Kobe, & Himeji

Kobe Beef: The Ultimate Splurge for Meat Lovers

Ask the Japanese what you should eat when you visit Kobe and the answer will invariably be *Kobe-gyu* (Kobe beef). Known for the flavor and tenderness of their meat, the cows, which come from an ancient line of Japanese cattle, are pampered almost beyond belief, receiving daily massages, sipping on saké and eating beer mash to keep their meat as perfectly marbled as possible. Not surprisingly, the luxurious bovine lifestyle doesn't come cheap, and it is consumers who pay the cost, with a dinner course of *Kobe-gyu* among the more expensive trips to a restaurant you'll find in Japan.

enough, Kitano-cho is popular mainly with domestic tourists. Of more interest to foreign visitors might be Kobe's small but lively **Chinatown** (Nankin-machi), about one kilometer south of Kitano-cho, next to Motomachi Station.

Continuing another 500 meters south from Motomachi leads to the harbor front and the very best of modern Kobe. Here, the waterfront **Harbor Land** redevelopment (harborland.co.jp) combines renovated brick warehouses, fine harbor

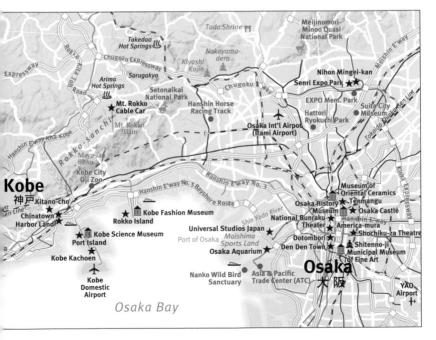

views, pleasant wooden walkways and numerous shopping and dining options, in many ways mimicking the harbor front area of Yokohama (page 38).

Heading offshore from here are two man-made islands in the bay, **Port Island** and **Rokko Island**. Rokko, built between 1973 and 1991, is home to many foreign businesses and expatriates, but the main reason to visit is the fantastic **Kobe Fashion Museum**, housed in a futuristic building that looks like it has just landed from Mars. Port Island, opened in 1981, has a pleasant bird and flower park (**Kobe Kachoen**), the worthwhile **Kobe Science Museum** (kobe-kagakukan.jp), and a good selection of shops and hotels.

Mount Rokko tram

Other Excursions in Kansai
A perfect fortress and a holy mountain

If you are going to be in Kansai for more than a few days, try and schedule some time out of the main cities. Best of all, book a night at one of the temples at **Koya-san** (see Japan's "Don't Miss"

The fire ceremony at Koya-san

Sights, page 23) and explore the holy mountain's sacred sites. Alternatively, head to **Himeji** (see Japan's "Don't Miss" Sights, page 20) in the west of Hyogo Prefecture, 50 kilometers (31 miles) from Kobe, a town known primarily for its castle, **Himeji-jo** (himeji-castle.gr.jp). Considered the archetypal feudal Japanese fortress, Hollywood has even used it as the backdrop to *The Last Samurai* and the Sean Connery-era James Bond film *You Only Live Twice*.

For something closer to Kobe, you could head north of Kobe for a nice soak in one of the natural hot springs at **Arima** (arima-onsen.com), where it is believed people have been bathing since Buddhist monks built a sanitarium in the area in the 8th century. Popular as a weekend retreat for people from Kyoto, Osaka and Kobe—in much the same way Hakone (page 39) is popular with Tokioites—Arima offers plenty of inns with hot spring baths that are perfect for soaking away the stresses of city life or relieving any aches and pains you might have from hiking the pretty 930-meter (2,953-foot) **Mount Rokko** just to the south.

Itsukushima's floating *torii* gateway

EXPLORING WESTERN JAPAN
From Hiroshima to the major islands of Shikoku and Kyushu

Heading west and south from Kansai, the tourist trail begins to thin out. Save for the travelers who pay their respects to the victims of the world's first atomic bombing in **Hiroshima** (see Japan's "Don't Miss" Sights, page 22) in the far west of Japan's main island, relatively few make it to the islands of **Shikoku** and **Kyushu**. Those who do are rewarded with some of Japan's best hot springs, glimpses of an ancient pilgrimage trail, the country's biggest dance festival and fine contemporary art.

Western Honshu
Hiroshima and Miyajima's "floating" shrine of Itsukushima

As western Honshu's most visited and Japan's most moving sight, the **Gempaku Dome** and related sites in **Hiroshima** (covered in detail in Japan's "Don't Miss" Sights, page 22) stand alone as a compelling reason to visit the far west of Japan's main island. The Hiroshima area, however, has more to it than reminders of Japan's first nuclear tragedy.

Comfortably visited as a day trip from Hiroshima, the small island of **Miyajima**, which can be reached from Hiroshima by a combination of train and ferry in about 45 minutes, is home to one of Japan's most distinctive spiritual sights—the "floating" *torii* gateway at **Itsukushima**

Shrine (miyajima-wch.jp). Some 16 meters (53 feet) in height and weighing about 60 tons, the *torii*'s two giant pillars were made using ancient camphor trees and a construction technique that allows them to stand unsupported on the sea bed. When the tide is high, and the gateway gives the impression of actually floating on the water, it's a truly spectacular sight, so much so that it has been designated as one of Three [most scenic] Views of Japan along with Matsushima Bay in Tohoku and the Amanohashidate sandbar in the far north of Kyoto Prefecture. When the tide is out and the *torii* stands naked in the midst of barren mud flats, however, spectacular gives way to underwhelming, so make sure you check tide times before visiting.

The gateway is currently in its 18th incarnation and is thought to have first been built here in the 12th century, almost 600 years after Itsukushima Shrine itself was founded. The main shrine, like so many of Japan's religious buildings, has been through numerous trials and tribulations over the centuries. The current structure, which combines orange-tinted wood with white walls to striking effect, dates to the 16th century and is based on 12th-century designs.

The Best of Shikoku
Pilgrims, feudal history and modern art

Though Shikoku is largely rural, with rugged capes at its southern end, deep gorges and lush valleys in its center (see Japan's Best Outdoor Activities, page 97) and farmland spread throughout, the first stop on the island for many visitors is urban, the main city of **Matsuyama**. Modern, but with a more relaxed vibe than most of Japan's larger cities, Matsuyama wears its rich history with pride. Its skyline is dominated by the historic and extensive **Matsuyama Castle** (matsuyamajo.jp) complex. The castle has been through several rebuilds since its initial construction in the 17th century by warlord Yoshiaki Kato, but the current version, perched upon a hill overlooking the city and Inland Sea, remains a daunting sight. Just as impressive is the series of reconstructed outer gateways near the end of the climb up to the main building, a walk steep enough to leave you wondering how anyone trying to storm the castle in full armor would have had

Western Japan

Shikoku's 88 Temple Pilgrimage Route

Pilgrims called *o-henro* have been visiting Shikoku for over 1,000 years to visit the 88 sacred sites associated with the Buddhist monk Kobo-Daishi (see Koya-san, page 23) that mark out a 1,400-kilometer (870-mile) tour of the island. Typically sporting white *oizuru* jackets and slacks and conical straw hats, with rosary beads, sutra book, bell and wooden staff, you'll mostly likely see them trudging between Shikoku's temples in spring and autumn when the weather is neither too hot nor too cold. Unlike in days gone by, when *o-henro* would walk the entire route, most modern-day pilgrims do the once-hard trek between temples in tour groups on comfortable air-conditioned buses, not surprisingly as most are of or near retirement age. The steps of Kotohira Temple (page 64) are one of the few occasions they will need to break into a sweat. Another occasion might be when they get home and calculate how much they have spent:

hotel fees, bus fees, temple donations, souvenirs and other pilgrimage expenses soon add up, even for those who take shortened tours to only the most famous of the 88 temples.

any energy left to fight by the time they reached the three-story donjon.

Once inside the castle, scale the almost vertical wooden staircases to the top floor for a panoramic view of downtown Matsuyama and Shikoku's northwest coast, then negotiate back down them (no mean feat) and take in the castle's fine collection of artifacts, which includes weaponry, scrolls and banners dating back to Kato's rule. The **Ninomaru Historical Garden** near the bottom of the hill on the way back down is also worth exploring for its ponds, waterfalls and rock features. It's not immediately noticeable, but study the garden carefully and you'll see its layout is a carbon copy of the palace floor plan.

The **Dogo Onsen** (dogo.or.jp), two kilometers by streetcar from central Matsuyama, lays claim to being the oldest hot spring in Japan; bathing here was first mentioned in the *Chronicles of Japan* some 1,300 years ago. The quarter's centerpiece, the Dogo Onsen Honkan, is a three-story wooden structure built in 1894. If it looks familiar, that could be because it was the inspiration for Hayao Miyazaki's bathhouse in the Oscar-winning animated film *Spirited Away*. Fans of Soseki Natsume might also have heard of the place. The novelist would bathe here during his stint teaching in Matsuyama, and the baths are where the eponymous main character in Soseki's book *Botchan* would come for a soak.

Although a dip in the baths today costs more than the eight sen Soseki would have paid in his day, little else seems to have changed. The Honkan retains its original baths, which become progressively more luxurious and expensive as you move up the floors. For ¥400, you can soak in the **Kaminoyu baths**, which are decorated with ornate heron mosaics. Pay ¥800 and you'll also be able to lounge about in a cotton *yukata* and take tea at the second-floor relaxation area. The most decadent experience can be found in the less-crowded **Tamanoyu baths** (¥1,200), where you can take in garden views and enjoy a more secluded area for tea and sweet "Botchan dango" dumplings after bathing.

On the other side of Shikoku, the fairly cosmopolitan city of **Takamatsu** is also worth a visit. Serving as the gateway to the "art island" of **Naoshima** and its brilliant contemporary art galleries and outdoor art installations (see Japan's "Don't Miss" Sights, page 21),

Takamatsu also boasts one of Japan's finest gardens, **Ritsurin** (see Japan's Parks and Gardens, page 101). The city can also be used as a staging post for visiting **Tokushima** to the southeast for the electrifying three-day **Awa-Odori** dance festival in August (see Festivals and Events, page 113) or for the far more peaceful **Kotohira** (town.kotohira.kagawa.jp) to the southwest, home to one of the most venerable stops on Shikoku's 88 temple pilgrimage (see previous page). Kotohira's mountaintop temple, **Kotohira-gu**, which is dedicated to the spiritual guardian of seafarers, is reached by 785 steps that leave many of its four million visitors out of breath. The effort is, however, well worth it. Once passed the first few hundred meters of tourist stalls, the climb takes you along increasingly peaceful tree- and stone lantern-lined pathways, passing an art museum and the temple's treasure house, before reaching the grand main temple building.

Ritsurin Garden in Takamatsu

The Best of Kyushu
Hot springs and primeval nature

Nagasaki Peace Park, site of the second atomic bomb

Kyushu, the western and southern-most of Japan's four main islands, attracts a different kind of tourist than those traveling to Tokyo and Kyoto. The island is heaving with volcanic activity and was the first point of entry for the Western "barbarians" in the 16th century. Even today, it has a blend of cultures and cuisine that make the island distinctly different.

The main city of **Fukuoka** is a rapidly growing cosmopolitan hub on the north of the island, with an international airport. Many visitors stay here for a day or two before traveling farther south to **Nagasaki,** a city that was the victim of the second atomic bomb attack during World War II. A hilly city facing the Ariake Sea, it is considered by Kyushu residents to be its most interesting city.

Overlooking Nagasaki Harbor is **Glover House**, completed in 1863 for the Scottish merchant Thomas Blake Glover (1838–1911) who lived there while helping early Japanese efforts to industrialize. The oldest "treaty port" wooden house surviving in Japan and notable for its blend of Western and Japanese elements, the single-story residence is surrounded by **Glover Garden**. (Open daily from 8 a.m. to 8 p.m.; Admission ¥610; glover-garden.jp/english) Other similar houses have been moved to the garden to preserve the city's foreign heritage, such as the Ringer House (1865) as well as the Nagasaki Masonic Lodge (1885).

Influences of the Portuguese, Chinese, Dutch and British traders still reverberate through the city. Although it was a port of entry for hundreds of years, non-Japanese were not allowed to mix with ordinary citizens and even today the city maintains a sort of exotic feel. This is reflected it its multicultural cuisine.

One confectionery for which Nagasaki is known is *castella*. The popular sponge cake was brought to Japan by Portuguese merchants in the 16th century. The name is derived from Portuguese Pão de Castela, meaning "bread from Castile." Sold in long narrow slices, it makes a fine treat with a cup of tea. *Chambon*, inspired by the cuisine of China, is made by frying pork, seafood and vegetables, but with a soup made with chicken and pork bones. Another specialty available in Chinatown is *shippoku*, which means table or tablecloth. A selection of many small dishes that combine Chinese, Japanese and Korean tastes are placed on a table and diners sample the array of dishes, transfering some to their plates.

Other Kyushu food ranges from potentially lethal blowfish (*fugu*) to some of the best *ramen* in the land. Originating from the Hakata district of Fukuoka, but now popular all over the country, *Hataka ramen*, in particular, combines a rich, creamy pork bone broth with thin but slightly chewy noodles, and can be topped with anything from sesame seeds and crushed garlic to pickled ginger.

A "hell pool" in Beppu

Traveling south and east from Fukuoka, the highway skims the towns of **Arita**, home of the famed Imari Porcelain ceramics, and **Kusatsu**, another pottery town which features subtle earthy glazes. Both towns are worth a visit, especially when they hold their annual pottery fairs.

The very best features of Kyushu, and the ones we focus on here, however, are natural. Continuing eastward, one must ascend **Mount Aso**, an active volcano in the center of the region that offers stunning vistas and ample opportunities for hiking. Still active, areas close to the volcano may be restricted when it is heaving with bilious gases, but the highlands around the rim are peaceful and green.

Descending Mount Aso brings visitors to the hot spring resort of **Yufuin**. Increasingly developed, what started out as a town with a few rustic and one very expensive inn, it now has many shops, museums, restaurants and baths open to the public. **Shitanyu**, open 10 a.m. to 10 p.m. (¥200), is the most accessible for travelers. Mount Yufu looms over the city and its residents feel that the mountain creates the same atmosphere as does Mount Hiei in Kyoto. (japan-guide.com)

It's only an hour from Yufuin to the east coast of Kyushu and the city of **Beppu**. The city sits on top of one of the most geothermically active regions on the planet, which in turn supplies the area's 3,000 or so hot springs with some 100 million liters (264 million gallons) of mineral-rich piping hot water every day. As a result, the town revolves around its *ryokan* (inns) and baths. With all the columns of white streams of steam emerging from the hotels, the town truly looks like Dante's vision of the entrance to hell (*jigoku*). Bathing in these "hell" baths is, of course, not allowed but they can be viewed. The red, green, white and blue cauldrons of boiling water are all separate pools but are beautifully landscaped with plantings that can survive the surrounding temperatures. (japan.apike.ca/japan_beppu_jigoku.html)

Another but more calming natural dimension to the town is Beppu's **sand baths**, something peculiar to the area (as well as farther south in Ibusuki), in which one is buried for 10 minutes in 40 degrees C (104 degrees F) sand that supposedly helps relieve ailments as diverse as neuralgia, muscle fatigue and indigestion. These bathing facilities are along the coast and although Kyushu is known for its noodles or Chinese influenced dishes, Beppu, facing the island of Honshu, reflects Honshu's pure Japanese tastes. For lovers of seafood, Beppu offers a fine selection of sushi shops and restaurants featuring fish.

Some 130 kilometers (80 miles) south of the southernmost city of Kagoshima are a pair of islands: **Tanegashima**, where Japan's Space Center is located, and **Yakushima Island** (see Japan's "Don't Miss" Sights, page 24), which gained World Heritage status as well as Ramsar designation for its unique flora and fauna.

EXPLORING HOKKAIDO
Asia's best skiing and much more on Japan's northernmost island

The northernmost of Japan's major islands, Hokkaido, was only settled by the Japanese in the 19th century and it remains in the minds of many Japanese something of a wild frontier, a vast expanse of land defined by its long harsh winters, rugged mountain ranges, dense forests, wetlands and rich farmland. Add Hokkaido's justified reputation for having some of Japan's heartiest regional foods, its finest skiing grounds in the shape of **Niseko** (see Japan's "Don't Miss" Sights, page 25), and a laid-back capital that oozes history, and you have a wonderfully distinct and unmissable experience waiting for you.

A Day in Sapporo
The capital of the rugged north

About 140 years ago, **Sapporo** was a frontier town tenaciously trying to carve out an existence in the Hokkaido wilderness. Now, with a population of 1.9 million, Japan's fifth biggest city is defined as much by its broad avenues as the mountain ranges on the skyline.

Unlike most Japanese cities, Sapporo is incredibly easy to get around, with streets laid out in a grid system that's centered on the pleasant green belt of **Odori Park** (Odori Koen) which runs east to west through the city center. It's here that the world-renowned **Sapporo Snow Festival** (page 111) is held over a week every February, when spectacular displays of giant snow and ice sculptures transform the city into a glistening outdoor gallery, in the process attracting almost two million people to Sapporo. Just east of Odori Koen, the **TV Tower** (tv-tower.co.jp) is a favorite with Japanese tourists, who

Sapporo Snow Festival ice sculptures

head to the tower's 90-meter (295-foot)-high observation deck to take in views of the city and mountains beyond. A few blocks north of the park, **Hokkaido University** (hokudai.ac.jp) is home to a fine botanical garden comprised of 5,000 different types of Hokkaido flora and fauna, as well as being the site of the **Batchelor Kinenkan** and its brilliant collection of artifacts relating to Hokkaido's indigenous people, the Ainu.

South of Odori Koen is where Sapporo comes alive at night, in the restaurants and bars around **Tanuki-koji** and the slightly seedier district of **Susukino**, where restaurants and bars rub shoulders with strip clubs and other adult venues. Don't let the latter put you off a walk around the area, especially if you like *ramen*. Susukino's **Ramen Yokocho**

Traditional warehouses along the canal in Otaru

(Ramen Alley), a narrow covered alley thick with the aroma of simmering chicken and pig bones and home to at least a dozen small *ramen* shops, is one of the best places in the city to slurp up a bowl of warming noodles. The other is the cleaner air of **Sapporo Ramen Republic** in the ESTA building (sapporo-esta.jp/ramen/), just outside Sapporo Station. This food court brings together eight *ramen* shops chosen to represent different parts of Hokkaido, ranging from versions of hearty Sapporo *miso ramen* to the light salty soup of the *shio ramen* from Morimachi in southern Hokkaido and a soy-based *ramen* from Asahikawa in the frozen center of the island. I don't normally get excited by *ramen*, but *miso ramen* in Sapporo, topped with corn and maybe a rich knob of Hokkaido butter, is worth the airfare to Hokkaido alone.

Touring Hokkaido
A taste of Japan's wild northern island

Y ou could spend weeks exploring all that Hokkaido has to offer, heading north and east to watch the ice floes of **Abashiri**, exploring the volcanic islands of **Rishiri** and **Rebun** or taking in the stunning surrounds of the UNESCO-designated **Shiretoko National Park** (shiretoko.or.jp) at the wild eastern tip of the island, not forgetting the multi-hued fields of lavender at Biei and Furano, the indigenous Ainu culture around Lake Akau and the seafood market at Kushiro. The list goes on and on.

For day trippers, the most popular excursion from Sapporo is the 30-minute train journey west to the harbor town of **Otaru** (otaru.gr.jp). The town's picturesque cobbled streets and canal, dotted with iron gaslights and carefully preserved 19th- and early 20th-century stone and brick buildings, point to Otaru's

The seafood market at Kushiro

former glory when it was a prosperous herring fishery and coal shipping port, with a thriving commercial and financial district dubbed the "Wall Street of the North." Today, the town is better known for its glasswork, and there are several glass factories and shops where you can make your own glass beads and other items. There is also a famous "Sushi Street" lined with excellent sushi restaurants. A closer option than Otaru, just 20 minutes east of central Sapporo, is the equally worthwhile **Historical Village of Hokkaido** (kaitaku.or.jp), an open-air museum housing 60 buildings relocated from around Hokkaido to create the effect of an early frontier town and to document the lives of Hokkaido's early pioneers.

Head 100 kilometers (62 miles) southwest of Sapporo and you will find Japan's premier ski grounds, **Niseko**, an area that also offers a multitude of outdoor activities in the summer months (see Japan's "Don't Miss" Sights, page 25, for more). Nearby, in the pristine Shikotsu-Toya National Park, lies **Noboribetsu** (noboribetsu-spa.jp), one of Hokkaido's best-known hot spring resort areas and the perfect place for a good hot soak. Another 40 kilometers (25 miles) to the northeast is the stunning scenery of **Lake Toya**, a caldera lake known in the indigenous Ainu language as Kimunto ("lake in the mountain") and an area of outstanding natural beauty.

Getting to Hokkaido

The main gateway to Hokkaido is Sapporo's New Chitose Airport. The new JR Tohoku/Hokkaido Shinkansen line also runs from Tokyo to Aomori and then under the sea to Hakodate, a journey of about four hours. From there, you can transfer to the Hokuto limited express to Sapporo, another three and a half hours. The entire trip costs about ¥23,000 one-way. A one-week Japan Rail Pass (covering the whole country at ¥29,110) or the JR Hokkaido Rail Pass (¥24,000) can also be used for this trip.

Ice floes near Abashiri

EXPLORING OKINAWA
Stunning nature and a distinctive culture

For most Japanese, Okinawa conjures up wonderful images of pristine beaches and dive spots, of tropical weather and a slower pace of life, and of a distinctive cuisine that at times borders on odd—all part of the rich Ryukyuan culture that makes the 70 or so islands collectively referred to as Okinawa so wonderfully and proudly different from the rest of Japan.

A Day around Naha
Discover the rich Ryukyuan culture

The main city on the main island of Okinawa, **Naha**, is where most visitors get their first taste of the Ryukyus,

on and around the main drag, **Kokusai-dori**, and in neighborhoods like the **Tsuboya pottery district**, where the 20 or so kilns in operation produce everything from the somewhat touristy *shisa* statues that are popular as souvenirs to fine ceramics. More than anything, Naha also affords the first opportunity to dive head first into Okinawan cuisine, from the pleasant bitter twang of *goya champuru* (a stir-fried mix of pork, egg, tofu and bitter gourd) and local takes on *soba* and *somen* noodles to the more challenging flavors of stewed *tonsoku* (pigs' trotters) and *mimiga* (vinegared pigs' ears). The latter pair might need to be washed down with a strong drink, in which case shun the usual saké and beer options for the local *awamori*, a distilled rice spirit weighing in at around 40% that can be taken on the rocks, with a little water or straight. There is no better way to take in the full spectrum of Okinawa's culinary sights and smells than with a walk around **Kosetsu Market**, a collection of covered shopping arcades extending off of Kokusai-dori.

Shuri Castle to the east of Naha

Getting out of the city center, heading east, the **Shuri district** is home to the main island's most historic and compelling site, **Shuri Castle** (oki-park.jp/shuri-jo-park), headquarters of the Japanese command during World War II. Situated in what's now called Shuri Castle Park, the site encompasses not just the rebuilt limestone castle and its gardens, mostly dating from 1992 after it was largely destroyed in the war, but also several structures and relics dating as far back as the 1500s when Shuri was the capital of the independent Ryukyu Kingdom, which remained independent until Okinawa become part of Japan in the 1870s.

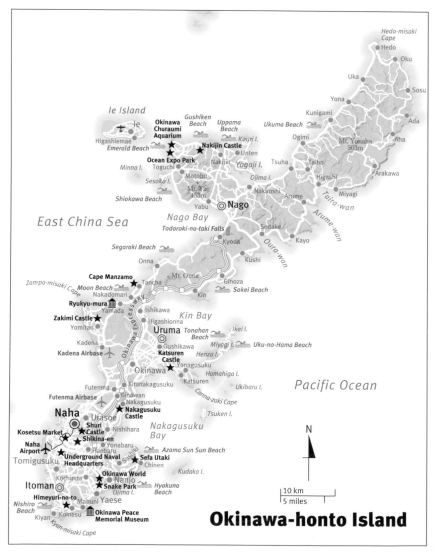

Okinawa-honto Island

Okinawa Churaumi Aquarium

Exploring Okinawa-honto
Fortress, beaches and marine life

Head north of Naha and there are many more worthwhile points of cultural and historic interest. You can find out more about Ryukyuan culture by visiting **Ryukyu-Mura** (ryukyumura.co.jp) to take in its preserved Okinawan farmhouses, watch the local Eisa dancing and learn about the islands' traditional weaving and dye crafts. Twenty minutes north of here, picturesque **Cape Manzamo**, near Onna Village, is famed for its unusual rock formation and picturesque setting facing the East China Sea. Further north, **Ocean Expo Park** (oki-park.jp) on the Motobu Peninsula on the northwestern coast, is another great place to learn more about local crafts and arts. Alongside a planetarium and museum focused on fishing communities, the park includes Japan's premier aquarium, **Okinawa Churaumi Aquarium**. Not only does Churaumi incorporate postcard-perfect beaches into its grounds, it includes sea turtle, manatee and dolphin pools and a variety of massive tanks brimming with colorful sea life; the biggest, with a capacity of 7,500 cubic meters (265,000 cubic feet), houses groups of manta rays and 9-meter (30-foot)-long whale sharks alongside 70 other species of fish.

South of Naha, World War II's impact on the island becomes increasingly visible. Some 140,000 Okinawans died during the brutal battles of Okinawa, as did more than 100,000 Japanese soldiers and 13,000 Americans. In many cases, the local civilians died by their own hand, rather than face the prospect of being captured by demonized American soldiers; perhaps the most heart-wrenching tale is that of **Himeyuri-no-to**, a deep pit at the southern tip of the island into which a group of high school girls and their teachers jumped to their death. This and many more stories from the Battle of Okinawa are told at the nearby **Okinawa Peace Memorial Museum**. Just east of Naha Airport, Tomigusuku offers another perspective on Okinawa during the war. Here you can visit the **Underground Naval Headquarters**, a labyrinth of tunnels and war rooms burrowed deep into the ground that will be familiar in style to anyone who has watched Clint Eastwood's *Letters from Iwojima*. Besides other tunnel networks, the large limestone caves that litter the southern part of the island were also where many locals sheltered during the heavy fighting, and you can explore parts of them at **Okinawa World** (gyokusendo.co.jp), about 10 kilometers (6 miles) southeast of Tomigusuku. Along with the caves, you will also find an unusual **Snake Park** and similar line-up of cultural attractions to Ryukyu-Mura.

Cape Manzamo

A short drive from Naha reveals more historical sights, namely the World Heritage Sites of the Gusuku Sites and Related Properties of the Kingdom of Ryukyu. The four most popular are Nakagusuku, Katsuren, Zakimi and Nakijin Castles. The castles' most prominent features are in the 14th-century stonework.

Start the trip at **Nakagusuku Castle**, built by the king Shou Taikyou's loyal retainer Gosamaru, who also built Zakimi Castle to the northwest. The castle was destroyed by Lord Amawari of **Katsuren Castle** (a half-hour drive away from Nakagusuku). Amawari had managed to convince the king Gosamaru was plotting a coup, but his treachery was later discovered and his own castle was attacked.

Zakimi Castle (40 minutes drive from Katsuren) features two inner courts with arched gates, and was used as a gun emplacement in World War II, which resulted in some of its walls being destroyed. These walls and foundations have since been restored. Rounding up the trip is **Nakijin Castle**, located on the Motobu Peninsula, with views of the East China Sea and one of the first places to see cherry blossoms each year. The castle housed several governing lords before it was eventually burned by the Japanese defending it from the Satsuma feudal domain in 1609. Some 1,500 meters (1,640 yards) of limestone castle remains.

Other Okinawan Islands
Sun-kissed beaches and eco-diversity

With almost 70 subtropical islands to choose from, stretching for 685 kilometers (425 miles), it can be difficult knowing where to start exploring beyond Okinawa. One of the closest, lying just 35 kilometers (22 miles) west of Naha, is **Zamami-jima** in the Kerama Islands, home to whale watching tours (late January through March) and the kind of white sand beaches postcard makers dream of. Snorkeling and scuba diving are among the top attractions. Moving much further afield, 300 kilometers (186 miles) south of Naha, there are equally stunning beaches in the Miyako group of islands, set amid coral reefs, most notably the 7-kilometer (4-mile)-long Maihama beach on **Miyako-jima**. This beach offers water sports, a sense of seclusion and the hypnotic combination of near white sand and emerald waters.

If you are feeling especially adventurous, travel to the **Yaeyama Islands** (see Japan's "Don't Miss" Sights, page 24) at the far southern end of the Ryukyus, and with it the southern and western boundaries of Japan. The islands here offer everything from pristine tropical beaches and mangrove swamps to traditional Okinawan villages and unique flora, fauna and wildlife.

CHAPTER 3
AUTHORS' RECOMMENDATIONS

Be it searching for a traditional Japanese inn or a restaurant to sample the finest *kaiseki* cuisine; knowing where to pick up the ideal souvenir or take in the most cutting-edge modern art; finding somewhere to wow the kids or the perfect park for some calm and quiet, Japan offers a wonderful but dizzying array of options. To help you cut through the clutter, here are our authors' picks for the best of the best in Japan.

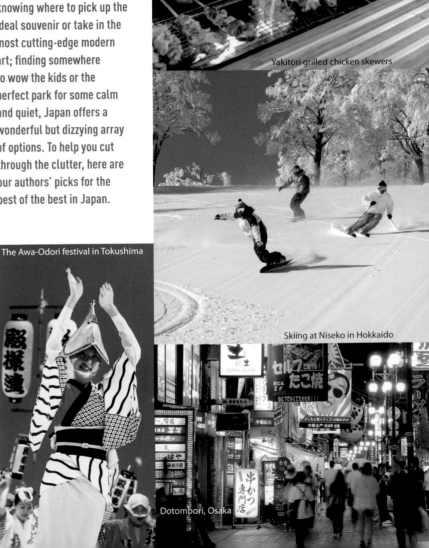

Yakitori grilled chicken skewers

The Awa-Odori festival in Tokushima

Skiing at Niseko in Hokkaido

Dotombori, Osaka

Japan's Best Hotels
Tokyo

Kanazawa

Kyoto

The Rest of Japan

Japan's Best Restaurants
Tokyo

Kyoto

Japan's Best Nightspots and Entertainment
Tokyo

Japan's Best Shopping
Tokyo

Kyoto

Japan's Best Outdoor Activities

Japan's Parks and Gardens

Kid-Friendly Attractions

Japan's Best Galleries and Museums

Tokyo Area

Kyoto

Osaka

Naoshima

Hiroshima

Festivals and Events

Winter

Spring

Summer

Autumn

JAPAN'S BEST HOTELS

A range of accommodation options from contemporary luxury to traditional elegance

From five-star modern luxury to traditional charms and even Zen, Japan's hotels and inns have all the bases covered. Here is a rundown of the very best accommodation options in Japan, plus some advice on where to book and budget options.

TOKYO

Mandarin Oriental

The Mandarin Oriental, Tokyo calls itself a "tower of contemporary luxury" for very good reason. Located on the upper floors of a skyscraper in Nihombashi, a short hop to Ginza in the center of Tokyo, the hotel boasts breathtaking city views that reach as far as Mount Fuji on a clear day, a pair of Michelin-starred restaurants,

the most indulgent day spa in Tokyo and sumptuously modern rooms. If you were going to max out a credit card for a single night in Tokyo, this would be the place to do it and still have a smile on your face when you get home. *mandarinoriental.co.jp*

Claska

For a city punctuated by so much cutting edge contemporary art and design, Tokyo is relatively lacking when it comes to stylish design hotels. The ones Tokyo does have, however, are simply stunning. And the Claska is the best of the lot. Situated in Shibuya Ward, a 5-minute taxi ride from Meguro Station, the hotel oozes sleekness through every pore, from the contemporary gallery on the 8th floor to the fashionable café-bar and, more importantly, the 16 rooms, which mix traditional Asian and Scandinavian sensibilities to create something distinctly modern and Japanese. *claska.com*

Park Hyatt

Let's get the clichéd bit out of the way first: this is the hotel where Bill Murray's character Bob stayed and drank in the

Mandarin Oriental, Tokyo

Park Hyatt, Tokyo

Sophia Coppola movie *Lost in Translation*. The bar in question, the 53rd-floor New York Bar, is one of Tokyo's most sophisticated cocktail spots and, like the rest of the Park Hyatt, commands tremendous views across the city center. Next door, the New York Grill is arguably the best hotel restaurant in Tokyo and comes with a wine collection second to none. As for the rooms, they are an enticing blend of classic and contemporary luxury—think green marble and granite mixed with dark woods—and feature every amenity you would expect in a 5-star hotel. *tokyo.park.hyatt.com*

Ritz Carlton

That the hotel sits atop the 53-story Tokyo Midtown urban development (page 10) speaks volumes of the Ritz Carlton, Tokyo's credentials. The Ritz is the definition of modern luxury, its 248 rooms and suites blending the contemporary designs of Frank Nicholson with panoramic views of the city that on clear days are accented by Mount Fuji (page 14) in the distance. And adding more five-star icing to that, the views are just as stunning from the Ritz's Michelin-starred restaurant and its ESPA-branded spa. *ritzcarlton.com*

Shigetsu Ryokan

Think traditional Japanese inn and most Japanese don't think Tokyo. While Kyoto and Japan's numerous hot spring areas are known for their *ryokan*, Tokyo's hotel scene is far more modern. Mostly. Located just off the colorful Nakamise-dori in Asakusa (page 9), and a short walk from all of Asakusa's main attractions, the Shigetsu is a great option for anyone looking for a traditional experience in the city. It boasts warm hospitality, rooms with *tatami* mat flooring and *futon* beds, a large communal bath, and a restaurant serving beautifully presented seasonal cuisine. *shigetsu.com*

Chinzanso

Located in Shinagawa Ward, the vast grounds and luxury of camellia-covered hills remains a surprise for guests that never imagine so much greenery can be found in the midst of this intensely populated city. Founded in 1861 during the Meiji era, the interior mixes Japanese and Western themes much as the newly established Meiji government did, as it attempted to incorporate Western culture

Japanese Business Hotels

Japan's "business hotels" represent a good budget option for travelers who don't want to stay in youth hostels. Nationwide chains like MyStays (mystays.com), Toyoko (toyoko-inn.com) and Dormy (hotespa.net), all have English-language booking websites, provide small but well-maintained and well-located rooms with a good range of amenities and free Wi-Fi. You will find branches of these and other chains in Tokyo, Kyoto, Hiroshima, Osaka and many other places covered in this book. Depending on the location, expect to pay between ¥4,000 and ¥8,000 per night for a single room and from ¥8,000 to ¥12,000 for a twin.

at the turn of the previous century. Every room is uniquely decorated with expansive views of the garden. *hotel-chinzanso-tokyo.com*

Grand Prince Takanawa

Located in Shinawaga, the recently renovated hotel boasts a large garden and numerous guest rooms, banquet facilities and restaurants. The reasonable prices make this an attractive hotel in this rather expensive city. *princehotels.com/takanawa*

KANAZAWA
Ana Crowne Plaza

A few minutes walk from Kanazawa Station, its reputation lies in its comfortable rooms, great views of the city, fine restaurants and high quality service. *anacrownplaza-kanazawa.jp/lang/english*

Asadaya Ryokan

This traditional inn fulfills everyone's expectation of the finest *ryokan* experience travelers can have. Gracious service and a beautiful, peaceful setting in downtown Kanazawa, the inn's history extends back centuries. The price per person includes two meals as is typical of Japanese inns. *asadaya.co.jp/ryokan*

Dormy Inn Natural Hot Spring

Although the rooms in this new chain of 3-star hotels are relatively small, the Dormy Inn offers a lot of comfort as well as a natural *onsen*. The rooftop bathing with washer and dryer units in the changing room area is much appreciated by dusty travelers who can do their own laundry while bathing. The inn is a 5-minute walk from Kanazawa Station but is a little hard to find without help. *hotespa.net/hotels/kanazawa*

Kaga Onsen

Kaga City Tourist Information Center inside the JR Kaga Onsen Station has a good listing of hotels and places to stay. A personal favorite is Yamashitaya Inn, not only because of its beautiful baths and reasonable prices but the buffet dinner allows visitors to eat as much or as little as they choose. *Tel: 0761-72-6678*

KYOTO
Hiragiya Ryokan

The perfect night in Kyoto would end here, drifting off to sleep after dining on the Hiragiya's sublime *kaiseki* cuisine eaten overlooking a pristine ornamental garden and soaking in one of the cypress wood baths. The Hiragiya is considered Kyoto's finest *ryokan* for good reason. The attention to detail, the service and the effortless precision of every moment are all impeccable. It's no wonder the Hiragiya has a guest book that reads like a Who's Who, with standout names from the *ryokan*'s near 200-year-old history, including Elizabeth Taylor and Charlie Chaplin. If you are going to splurge on a single night for the ultimate traditional Japanese experience, splurge here. *hiragiya.co.jp*

Hiiragiya Ryokan, Kyoto

Hyatt Regency, Kyoto

Hyatt Regency

With 189 rooms designed by renowned Japanese design house Super Potato, the Hyatt Regency in the eastern side of the city is Kyoto's answer to Tokyo's slew of high-end modern hotels. Combining sleek contemporary décor with traditional design elements such as *washi* paper fittings and kimono fabric headboards, Super Potato have pulled off a design classic, which the Hyatt has added to with highly rated Japanese and Italian restaurants serviced by a highly competent multilingual staff. The Hyatt is worth each of its five stars.
kyoto.regency.hyatt.com

Hotel Kanra

Hotel Kanra is the epitome of "small is beautiful." The boutique hotel's soft lighting, modern Japanese décor and comfort is located next to Higashi Hongan-ji temple, a 12-minute walk from Kyoto Station. The rooms have Japanese *tatami* flooring that softens one's footfall and Japanese-style wooden bathtubs for a traditional and soothing soak. Both Japanese-style and Western-style breakfasts are available. Teppanyaki and Italian cuisine is served in the attached restaurant. The hotel provides concierge services and luggage storage. *hotelkanra.jp/en*

Four Seasons

Located in the Eastern foothills, views from the hotel's 123 rooms include the 800-year-old pond and garden against a backdrop of temple rooftops. An expansive outside deck overlooks the hotel's extensive stroll garden. The Shakusei-tei tearoom serves traditional bowls of whipped powdered green tea during the day and flutes of champagne in the evenings. The spa and fitness rooms are well appointed with a 24-hour fitness center for cardio and weight training besides the 20-meter (65-foot) indoor pool and separate whirlpool. From the entrance, one sees evidence of traditional craftsmen. The wooden umbrella-like structure that allows guests to alight from taxis is a unique piece of ancient carpentry skill. *fourseasons.com/kyoto/*

Ritz Carlton

Situated directly beside the Kamo River, the elegant and spacious rooms overlook the river and the Eastern Mountains or the city. The location is a 10-minute walk from the downtown area via the city streets or along the riverside making a simple stroll into a scenic journey.

Designed to resemble the quiet dimly lit journey into Japanese traditional inns, the interior décor reflects the stillness that marks the city's old inns. But the resemblance ends when entering the elegant and light-filled rooms. Sleek black-lacquered counters with golden fixtures bring an added touch of refinement. The fitness center includes a lap pool and spa facilities. The Italian dining room is situated in a renovated century's old building. The more modern Japanese dining room serves traditional Japanese *kaiseki*, *teppanyaki*, *sushi* and *tempura*. A 15-minute taxi ride from Kyoto Station, a 3-minute walk from the Shiyakusho-mae subway station. *ritzcarlton.com*

Suiran

Nestled against the Western mountains and beside the scenic Hozu River in Arashiyama is the small, intimate, 39-room hotel offering guests a retreat from the city center. This was the old estate of Baron Shozo Kawasaki of Kawasaki Steel who built his summer home along the river that slices through the narrow gorge plied with narrow, shallow bottomed boats carrying visitors who come to enjoy the spectacular mountainside scenery and cool breezes in summer. His traditional wooden home has been converted into the dining room, serving Japanese food. The hotel can be reached by a 2-minute taxi ride from JR, Hankyu and Keifuku rail lines or a 35-minute taxi ride from Kyoto Station. *suirankyoto.com/en*

Shunko-in Temple

Located in one of the subtemples of the mighty Myoshinji Temple complex comprising 47 subtemples in northwest Kyoto, this peaceful *shukubo* (temple lodging) is not only an absolute gem, it's one of the most affordable places to stay in Kyoto. Everything here is no-frills. There are no meals but there is a well-equipped shared kitchen; the simple but smart rooms mostly come with just a *futon* and free Wi-Fi; and unlike many temple lodgings there are no restrictions on when you can come and go. What makes Shunko-in really special is the hospitality of the English-speaking vice abbot, the Rev. Kawakami, and his family, not to mention its proximity to Ryoan-ji, Kinkaku-ji and other must-see sights. On top of that, it's just so quiet and calm, the perfect atmosphere for taking part in the daily meditation sessions the Rev. Kawakami conducts in English. *shunkoin.com*

Hotel and Ryokan Booking Sites

The listings in this section focus on a small and select number of hotels and *ryokan* that represent the best of the best and are fully accessible to English speakers. You can, however, find and book many more great *ryokan*, hotels and hostels online in English. If you want something traditional, the Japan Ryokan Association (ryokan.or.jp) is a good first stop and also has useful information on how *ryokan* operate, *ryokan* etiquette and the like. For bookings across the board, the reliable Rakuten Travel site (travel.rakuten.com) lists more than 5,000 hotels and *ryokan*. The equally trustworthy Japanican.com has over 4,000 listings as well as a great line-up of tours and cultural experience options.

Shunko-in Temple

THE REST OF JAPAN

Fujiya Hotel, Hakone

Hakone has plenty of good *ryokan* to choose from (see page 82 for booking sites), but at the risk of sounding like a football chant, there is only one Fujiya Hotel. Opened in 1868 as Japan's first Western-style resort, in its heyday the Fujiya attracted a stream of foreign celebrities and dignitaries. Charlie Chaplin stayed here. So did King George IV before taking the throne. John Lennon, Yoko Ono and son Sean were regulars. The current Emperor and Empress are in the guest book as well. Photos of them and many others adorn the old wooden hallways of the main building, which along with the attached *ryokan* (Kikka-so) is now registered as an Important Cultural Asset. Today, the celebs stay elsewhere but the Fujiya still emits an old-world charm from every pore, from the high-ceilinged dining hall where chefs produce sublime French courses through to the bar where John Lennon used to play the grand piano. It's like staying in a museum. *fujiyahotel.jp*

Dinner at Eko-in Temple, Koya-san

Fujiya Hotel, Hakone

Eko-in Temple, Koya-san

This is accommodation the Zen way. As is typical with *shukubo* (temple lodging), there's nothing flash about the accommodation at this temple near Koya-san's Okuno-in cemetery, just a *tatami* mat room with low table, *futon* mattress and small TV, plus communal washrooms. But that's exactly the point. This is all about experiencing (in part, at least) life as a monk. If you ask me, the monks don't have it bad at all. The in-room meals are beautifully presented mini *kaiseki* affairs. The communal wooden bath is as inviting as anything at a good *ryokan*. And it's well worth getting up early for the spectacular prayer sessions. They begin at 6.30 a.m. sharp in the incense-thick inner temple as the monks recite sutras with hypnotic, droning chanting that's driven on by pounding drum beats. Then they move to a smaller building, reaching a fiery crescendo as a single monk burns 108 pieces of wood representative of the 108 defilements to be overcome on the road to enlightenment. *ekoin.jp*

Benesse House, Naoshima

Fancy staying in an internationally acclaimed art gallery designed by a pre-eminent Japanese architect? On a tranquil art-filled island in the Seto

Benesse House, Naoshima

Inland Sea? Then it has to be Benesse House on Naoshima. Designed by Tadao Ando and operated by the Benesse publishing group, the coastal grounds of this super sleek hotel (think smooth concrete, cavernous spaces and angular designs that blend perfectly with the rugged island terrain) are peppered with art installations, while the galleries inside and even many of the rooms feature works by acclaimed contemporary artists from around the world. Add to that the holistic spa, the chance to wander the museum's exhibits 24 hours a day and the ocean views from each room, and it's close to being the perfect luxury retreat. *benesse-artsite.jp/benessehouse*

Hilton Niseko Village, Niseko

Located at the southern foot of scenic Niseko Annupuri Mountain, affording the luxury of ski-in and ski-out access to some of Japan's finest skiing, the Niseko Village has taken "prime location" to a new level. It doesn't do badly on the luxury front either, with a good range of dining options, an après-ski bar warmed by an open hearth, smartly designed rooms with sweeping mountain views and an outdoor hot spring bath that's perfect for soaking in the views and soaking out the sporting aches. When the snow has gone, the proximity to hiking and biking trails and white-water rafting or canoeing, not to mention the 18-hole golf course next door, make it just as appealing. *niseko-village.com*

Busena Terrace Beach Hotel, Okinawa

When the year 2000 Economic Summit was held in Japan, this hotel was selected as the site of that historic event because of its beautiful scenery, fine facilities and ocean views. The combination of fine restaurants and the nearby beach make it a prime choice for visitors to the island. The outdoor pools and terraces are a luxurious venue for those who really want to relax in true resort style. There is also a full-service spa to further that goal. The resort is a 5-minute walk to the beach and Busena Marine Park. Free WiFi service and Internet service are available in all 410 rooms as well as 24-hour room service. *terrace.co.jp/en*

Ritz Carlton, Okinawa

For years, the only thing Okinawa lacked to go along with its 5-star beaches and alluring culture were top-notch accommodation options. Yes, there have always been plenty of resorts but nothing on a par with the very best travelers could find in Southeast Asia or the Pacific Islands. Not any more. And nothing represents that better than the Ritz Carlton's 97-room property on the main island's Motobu Peninsula. Positioned next to an 18-hole championship golf course and with views out over the East China Sea, the Ritz is 5-star from its indulgent ESPA spa and highly rated Teppanyaki restaurant all the way through to its sleekly designed rooms and suites. *ritzcarlton.com*

JAPAN'S BEST RESTAURANTS

Discover what makes Japan a foodie's paradise

A Japanese-style pub restaurant (*izakaya*)

Whether slurping up a quick bowl of *ramen* or setting in for the long haul of a multicourse *kaiseki* dinner, the Japanese absolutely love their food. In this nation of gourmands, you'll find restaurants of some kind or other almost everywhere you go (Tokyo alone has 100,000!), and mostly they will be good at the very least. Although many won't have English-language menus or English-speaking staff, you'll find plenty that have plastic mock-ups of their dishes in their window displays and others with picture menus, so language barriers don't have to get in the way of a good feed. What follows is a select few of the very best Japanese restaurants in Kyoto and Tokyo that are accessible to non-Japanese speakers, plus suggestions for types of food to look out for elsewhere.

TOKYO
Tofuya Ukai

This mock Edo-era mansion in the shadow of Tokyo Tower provides the perfect setting for the most exquisitely presented and sublimely flavored tofu-based *kaiseki* cuisine in Tokyo. Taken in *tatami* mat rooms that overlook a beautifully ornate Japanese garden, the courses here run through multiple small yet sumptuous dishes. You might begin with starters like grilled bamboo shoots served with rape blossoms and sea bream in *sakura* leaves, then progress to creamy tofu blocks sim-mered in soy milk and deep-fried tofu with sweet miso dressing. And it will all be served with the refinement and precision for which Japan is famed. Reservations essential. ***ukai.co.jp***

Tomoegata

There's good reason why sumo images adorn the flags standing outside this always busy restaurant in Ryogoku. Located just a 5-minute walk from Japan's main sumo stadium, the Kokugikan, Tomoegata specializes in *chanko nabe,* the hearty stew sumo wrestlers eat to bulk up. There's nothing better on a chilly night than picking away at the steaming *chanko* as its simmers along in a big hotpot at the center of your table. And if that isn't enough to make you punch new holes in your belt, they also serve great *sashimi* (raw fish) and other side dishes that wouldn't be out of place in a good *izakaya*. Reservations essential if you come on the day of a sumo tournament. ***tomoegata.com***

Fukuzushi

In business since 1917 and now in the hands of master *sushi* chef George Fukuzawa, Fukuzushi combines every-thing you'd expect from a traditional Japanese restaurant—impeccable service and hospitality and beautiful presentation of both food and interiors—with modern

MUST-TRY JAPANESE FOODS

Japan has such an array of traditional dishes and regional specialties that knowing what kind of restaurant to opt for can be even more challenging than navigating a handwritten Japanese-language menu. Here are some of Japan's very best foods and suggestions on where to try them.

KAISEKI-RYORI Featuring many small yet immaculately presented dishes that showcase seasonal produce, *kaiseki* is Japanese cuisine at its most refined and most expensive. Not only are the flavors sublime, so too is the experience, from the tranquil *tatami* mat dining room and attentive kimono-clad waitresses to the fine china and lacquerware on which the dishes are served. It is culinary perfection. See the Kyoto listings on pages 87–9 for places to try *kaiseki*.

SUSHI The cuisine itself needs no introduction, but where is the best place to try it? If you are on a budget, look for a *kaiten-zushi* (conveyor belt-style) *sushi* shop like the Heiroku-zushi chain in Tokyo or try breakfast at one of the many small, reasonably priced restaurants around Tokyo's Tsukiji Market (page 11). If budget is no concern, go to Fukuzushi (page 85) in Tokyo for a truly sumptuous meal.

NOODLES Japan has a great love of noodles. None are as popular as *ramen*, for which regional variations abound (none

Ramen noodles

better than Sapporo's *miso ramen*, page 69). Japan's love affair with noodles is such that people will happily queue for hours for a few blissful minutes of *ramen* slurping at the most lauded restaurants. Less revered but no means lesser, *soba* (buckwheat) noodles are equally wonderful served chilled in summer and dipped in a light soy-based sauce or served in a hot broth and topped with battered and deep-fried *tempura* seafood and vegetables in winter. *Udon*, a thick wheat flour noodle, is just as versatile. You can have it chilled or in a broth or use it to bulk up a *nabe* (hotpot). You will find *ramen*, *udon* and *soba* restaurants everywhere, the cheapest (with prices often under ¥300) being the stand-up *soba* and *udon* outlets in and around many train stations.

B-KYU GURUME "B-grade cuisine" has been enjoying a renaissance in Japan in recent years. No frills and low cost, *b-kyu* includes everything from the Osaka favorite *okonomiyaki* (a kind of meat, fish and vegetable-packed pancake) to *yakitori* (grilled chicken skewers). In Osaka, Dotombori (page 56) is a great place to find *okonomiyaki* joints, while there is a street packed with great rough and ready *yakitori* places several blocks west of Senso-ji in Asakusa (page 9). If you fancy some *b-kyu* that is distinct to Tokyo, try the *monjayaki* in Tsukishima (page 31).

Sushi

touches that include a café-bar lounge. All these, of course, would be worthless if the food wasn't up to scratch. And at Fukuzushi you get *sushi* at its very best, the restaurant sourcing the finest seasonal produce from Hokkaido and serving up delicacies such as melt-in-the mouth *o-toro* (tuna belly cut), *ikura* (salmon roe) that delicately pops on the tongue, and *aji* (horse mackerel) topped with spring onion, *wasabi* and ginger. Reservations essential. *roppongifukuzushi.com*

Inakaya

This excellent *robatayaki* restaurant in the up-market Roppongi district of has become a regular fixture in guidebooks and travel brochures. Fine traditional food meets pure theater here. The rustic wooden interior and the grilled seafood and skewers of meat make you feel as if you have stopped off for dinner in deepest rural Tohoku, while the way the tradition-ally dressed waiting staff scream your orders to the chefs, who scream back even louder before delivering your food across the counter on the end of a 2-meter (6-foot) paddle, could have come straight from the old theaters of Asakusa. Reser-vations essential. *roppongiinakaya.jp*

Kisoji

This 70-year-old restaurant in Akasaka serves *shabu shabu*: thin slices of beef and pork (along with a variety of seasonal vegetables) that you cook in a hotpot at your table then dip in a choice of sauces. What makes this place different to the numerous other *shabu shabu* restaurants around town—besides the fantastic qual-ity of the meat—is that it goes all out on the traditional touches (think *tatami* mat flooring and ornamental rock garden) to create an incredibly refined experience. Reservations essential.
kisoji.co.jp/kisoji/english

Ise Sueyoshi

Here, a great variety of food cultures come into play with an overriding Japanese theme and offering a great selection for its guests. Imaginative Japanese, Asian, vegetarian-friendly, vegan and gluten-free options are among what is available. The chef trained at the Michelin-star restaurant Kikunoi in Kyoto, bringing the sensitivity of Kyoto *kaiseki* to Tokyo. Closed Friday and Sunday. Open 5.30 p.m. to 11.00 p.m.
isesueyoshi.blog.fc2.com

Torafuku

This restaurant enjoys pride of place in that it specializes in Koshihikari rice from Niigata Prefecture. The huge hearth in the center of the wooden interior exudes the warmth of a home-cooked meal. There is a large selection of rice dishes available with sides of fish, soup and pickles and, of course, saké to en-hance the very reasonably priced meal. Open 11.30 a.m. to 11.30 p.m.
our-seeds.co.jp (in Japanese)

KYOTO
Ikkyu

You don't need to stay at a temple to sam-ple *shojin-ryori*, the vegetarian fare eaten by monks. Situated just outside the south-east entrance to the Daitoku-ji temple complex (page 51), this business has been in the same family for nearly half a millennium and over that time they have perfected the art of vegetarian *kaiseki*. Ordinarily simple tofu and seasonal vege-tables are transformed into mini gastro-nomical masterpieces that are enhanced by the setting. Meals here are taken sit-ting at low tables on *zabuton* cushions with views across a traditional temple garden. Reservations essential.
daitokuji-ikkyu.jp

Kaiseki cuisine

Kikunoi

Subtle yet distinct describes the delicacies that appear on your table at this world-renowned restaurant. Regarded as the apex of Kyoto hospitality and refined taste, Kikunoi (the name means "chrysanthemum well") presents dishes in which taste rivals beauty of the service and atmosphere. Located in downtown Kyoto, your meal there will be memorable. Reservations necessary. The slow graceful pace of service means that all *kaiseki* meals take approximately over an hour and the reason for the early entry date below. Open 11.30 a.m. to 1 p.m. and 5 p.m. to 8 p.m. (last entry). *kikunoi.jp/english/*

Karyo

Kaiseki is Japan's haute cuisine. The multi-course meal is the bountiful result of labor-intensive preparations that include steamed, grilled, fried, boiled and uncooked dishes served on exquisite ware. Each dish is a celebration of this labor and the beautiful presentation makes Karyo worth a visit. Situated on the main street of Hanami-koji that cuts through the Gion district, the restaurant

is a 10-minute walk from the downtown intersection of Shijo-dori and Kawamachi-dori, and situated directly across from Gion Kaburenjo Theater. Lunch (8-dish lunch set) ¥5,000; dinner (9-dish dinner sets) ¥10,000–¥30,000. Prices do not include tax and service charge. Major credit cards are accepted. Open every day except Wednesday. Lunch 11.30 a.m. to 5.30 p.m.; dinner 6 p.m. to 11 p.m. *karyo-kyoto.en*

Tempura Yoshikawa

When done right, *tempura* (deep-fried seafood and seasonal vegetables) is magical. Few restaurants do it better than Tempura Yoshikawa. Located within a high-end *ryokan* (the Yoshikawa Inn) in a beautiful 100-year-old building, this *tempura* restaurant offers diners the choice of eating their multi-dish course in a private *tatami* mat room (some of which overlook the inn's lovely garden) or watching the chefs at a sunken *tempura* counter that seats just 12. Whichever you choose, the atmosphere is intimate and truly "old Kyoto." This being Kyoto, you don't just get *tempura* here (a good thing, too, as dish after

Kobe beef

dish of deep-fried food would be hard to take!). Instead, the courses blend traditional seasonal *kaiseki* dishes with unbelievably light *tempura* that includes wonderfully textured shrimp and the freshest of in-season vegetables.
kyoto-yoshikawa.co.jp

Ashiya Steak House

Tucked away on a back alley near the Yasaka Shrine district, this restaurant offers some of the best cuts of Kobe beef available. An old-style rickshaw stands before the entrance of Ashiya Steak House and the honey-colored wooden interior and gracious service contribute to make any meal here a memorable experience. The upstairs gallery features woodblock-cut prints by Clifton Karhu along with the photographs of the notable customers who have visited here over the years.
steak-house-ashiya.com (in Japanese)

Ramen Alert

For the many aficionados of this curly noodle soup, a trip to the 10th floor of the Kyoto Station should satisfy all appetites. There are nine shops specializing

in *ramen* from all different parts of the country, so get your chopstick skills up to par. Open 11 a.m. to 10 p.m. (last order 9.30 p.m.) *ramen-koji.com*

Snoopy Café

Everyone knows that Hello Kitty is Japan's top cat, and a new Hello Kitty store is located on the north side of Shijo-dori a little west of Kawaramachi. But not as many know of the Japanese love of Snoopy. This famous beagle has arrived in Kyoto. The gift shop on Nishiki Market street not only sells goods but food items made in the shape of this famous character. The second-floor restaurant offers dishes that kids love, with Snoopy's image appearing in each. The bane of many a Japanese mother is to produce a box lunch that will tempt and delight the young eater. Snoopy is the latest comic book icon to receive this treatment and this shop offers a great look at the Japanese food mentality of making food as attractive (or as cute) as possible.

Useful Restaurant Phrases

Do you have an English menu? *Eigo no menyuu ga arimasu ka?*
What do you recommend? *O susume wa nan desu ka?*
Can I have (some water)? *(Mizu) o onegai shimasu?*
Can I have this, please? (said when pointing to something) *Kore o onegai shimasu.*
It's tasty! *Oishii desu!*
Cheers! *Kampai!*
Could I have the bill, please? *O-kaikei o onegai shimasu?*
Thank you for the meal (said to staff when leaving a restaurant or to people at your table when finishing your meal) *Gochisosama deshita.*

JAPAN'S BEST NIGHTSPOTS AND ENTERTAINMENT

Urban Japan bristles with energy through the night

Classic theater, cool bars and all-night dancing are just a few of the evening entertainments on offer in Japan's main cities. So whether you want to take in a *kabuki* play, sip saké or dance till dawn, here is the lowdown on the best places to do it in Tokyo, Kyoto and Osaka.

TOKYO
Bars and Pubs

For a good drink combined with good food, there are *izakaya* at every turn in Shinjuku, Shibuya, Shimbashi and most other central areas. Many will require some Japanese-language skills to read the menus and order, so one option is to try a chain *izakaya* with picture menus, like Shirokiya and Watami, where you can point and smile to order. Shinjuku's infamous **Kabuki-cho** red-light district is definitely worth exploring, perhaps to experience the out-of-this-world nightclub show at the **Robot Restaurant**, which is unforgettably weird. Another option is to head to **Shin-Hinomoto** (aka Andy's) under the elevated rail tracks in Yurakucho, a classic *izakaya* with a slight twist; it's run by an Englishman who is happy to talk you through the menu. For something a bit more specialized, beer geeks will want to grab a pint or eight at the chicly designed **Goodbeer Faucets** (goodbeerfaucets.jp) in Shibuya or the more homely **Beer Club Popeye** in Ryogoku (beeradvocate.com) to sample Japan's booming and brilliant craft beer industry. Both pubs have extremely knowledgeable English-speaking staff and an incredible lineup of brews; there are 70 taps at Popeye and 40 at Goodbeer. For something more up-market, all the major international hotels have good bars that are well versed in catering to English speakers. For one of the best, head to the Park Hyatt (page 78) in Shinjuku for a cocktail or fine wine at the swanky 53rd-floor **New York Bar**.

The raucous Robot nightclub show

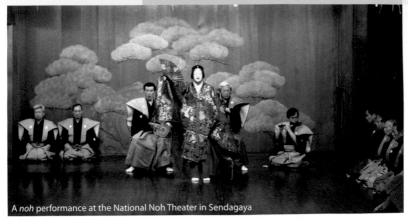

A *noh* performance at the National Noh Theater in Sendagaya

Clubs and Live Music

As with its bars, Tokyo has a dizzying lineup of great live music venues and clubsthat combine to cater to every taste. Among the best **dance clubs** are **Womb** (womb.co.jp) and **Dommune** (dommune. com) in Shibuya and **Ageha** (ageha.com) in Shin Kiba. The live music scene ranges from supper jazz clubs like the internationally renowned **Blue Note** (bluenote.co.jp) in Aoyama to **Billboard Live** in Tokyo Midtown (page 10), and the **Cotton Club** in Marinouchi to big rock and pop venues such as **Tokyo Dome** (where the Yomiuri Giants play baseball) and more intimate "live houses" like **Crocodile** (crocodile-live.jp) and **Club Quattro** (club-quattro.com) in Shibuya. For a full round-up of entertainment options, see *Time Out Kyoto* (timeout.jp/en/kyoto) and the *Kyoto Visitor Guide* (kyotoguide.com).

Traditional Entertainment

After a long hiatus, the **Kabuki-za Theater** (kabuki-za.co.jp) has been rebuilt and reopened and is once again Tokyo's premier *kabuki* venue, with regular performances that come accompanied by English-language audio guides. The **Shimbashi Embujo** (shochiku.co. jp/play/enbujyo) in Higashi-Ginza, that took on the mantle of Tokyo's main *ka-*

buki theater while Kabuki-za was out of action, still puts on regular performances. The **National Theater** (ntj.jac.go.jp) in Hanzomon is also good for *kabuki* as well as *bunraku* (puppet theater), *buyo* (dance), *gagaku* (court music), *hogaku* (music) and *minzoku geino* (folk performing arts). For other traditional performing arts, try the **National Noh Theater** (ntj.jac.go.jp) in Sendagaya for *noh* and *kyogen* with English guidance.

For something very Japanese but more modern, stop by a **karaoke** box and unleash your inner diva. You'll find places all over Tokyo (and other towns and cities) where you and your friends can rent a small private room and order food and drink to accompany the singing. **Smash Hits** (smashhits.jp) in Hiroo is a favorite for expats, while the **Big Echo** chain (big-echo.jp) has thousands of English songs available.

KYOTO

Like Tokyo, Kyoto has plenty of great options for drinking, clubbing and listening to live music. (See Time Out's Kyoto listings for a full round-up of options: timeout.jp/en/kyoto). But where the city really excels is with traditional performing arts like *kabuki* and *noh*. For the heavily stylized dance-drama *kabuki*,

A *bunraku* puppet play at Gion Corner Theater

head to the **Minami-za** theater (kabuki-bito.jp/eng) on Shijo-dori. This charmingly restored Edo-era playhouse is the oldest *kabuki* venue in Japan and attracts the biggest performers in the field. For *noh*, try the **Kanze Kaikan** (kyoto-kanze.jp) in Okazaki, which hosts about a dozen performances of these classical, slow-moving musical dramas each month.

If you have the urge to take in as many different performing arts as you can with a single visit, try **Gion Corner Theater** (kyoto-gioncorner.com). For some people the hour-long review here, which features snippets of *bunraku* (puppetry), *chado* (tea ceremony), *gagaku* (court music), *ikebana* (flower arranging), *koto* (Japanese harp), *kyogen* (comic acting) and *kyomai* (dancing), is a little too touristy but for others it's the perfect introduction to a wealth of quintessentially Japanese traditional arts.

A new venue is **Ran** (rankyoto.com), which showcases 90 minutes of dynamic, traditional folk music on the *shamisen*, *koto* and *nohbue* transverse flute, as well as Japanese *taiko* drums.

OSAKA

The old merchant city of Osaka has a well-deserved reputation for lively nightlife, and the Dotombori and Shinsaibashi areas, in particular, are packed with many good bars, *izakaya* and restaurants. If you get the urge to dance, and you like a mix of musical styles, **Joule** (club-joule.jp) in Shinsaibashi is a popular choice, while **Club Karma** in Kita-ku pumps out drum 'n bass and techno. The live music scene includes high-end venues like the **Billboard Live Osaka** (billboard-live.com) in Umeda, which attracts top international jazz and R&B acts, and the rock- and indie-focused **Club Quattro** (club-quattro.com) in Umeda, but also has smaller, more intimate venues like the very hip restaurant-bar-club **Café Absinthe** (absinthe-jp.com). Japan has some excellent magicians found at **magiclabjapam.com**.

For some traditional entertainment, Dotombori also delivers. The **National Bunraku Theater** (ntj.jac.go.jp), where the focus is on puppet theater, and the **Shochiku-za Theater** (kabuki-bito.jp), where the emphasis is on *kabuki*, are both wonderful venues offering authentic performances in shorter periods.

Dotombori, Osaka

JAPAN'S BEST SHOPPING

Get ready to max out your credit card!

Shops and cafés inside Omotesando Hills

Be it perusing brand name boutiques or rummaging through flea markets, Japan is a shopper's paradise with great shopping options to suit all budgets. Here is a rundown on where to shop in Tokyo and Kyoto, by far the best two cities for a spot of retail therapy on your trip to Japan.

TOKYO
Fashion

With several of Tokyo's most prestigious **department stores** (in the shape of Mitsukoshi, Matsuya, Matsuzakaya and Wako), not to mention sleekly designed **flagship stores** for a Who's Who of high-end European brands (think Bulgari, Cartier, Chanel, Tiffany and more), **Ginza** can rightly lay claim to being Tokyo's premier shopping district for fashion and style. Those brands naturally have given Ginza something of a high-cost reputation, but Ginza also offers large branches of affordable fashion brands such as Gap,

Designer stores in Ginza

Zara, Muji and Uniqlo, making the area popular with shoppers of all budgets.

Rivaling Ginza as Tokyo's premier shopping area, the kilometer-long main street in **Omotesando** (page 32) is lined by high-end European fashion boutiques and dominated by the Tadao Ando-designed **Omotesando Hills** mall (page 32) that stretches along almost a third of the street's length. At the northwest end of Omotesando, near Harajuku Station, the narrow and always crowded **Takeshita-dori** adds a different dimension to the area. It's here that you'll find numerous small boutiques catering to teen fashions as well as goth and cosplay tastes. A station away from Harajuku, shopping in **Shibuya** is also firmly centered on youth. In the eight-story **Shibuya 109 Building** (shibuya109.jp), in particular, there are more than 100 boutiques selling all manner of cosmetics, fashions and accessories, while the **Center Gai** area (now officially called Basketball Street, though nobody seems to call it that) is another good place for exploring small youth-focused stores. Catering to a wider demographic, Shibuya also has the Seibu, Parco and Tokyu department stores. You'll also find several good department stores, such as Isetan and Marui, in **Shinjuku**, along with a very broad mixture of other stores, from ubiquitous budget fashion chains

Akihabara, the place to be for *manga, anime*, game and electronics enthusiasts

such as Uniqlo and Muji to major home electronics department stores such as Yodobashi and Biku Camera. With several hundred stores spread around the ultramodern **Roppongi Hills** (page 10) and **Tokyo Midtown** (page 10) developments, **Roponggi** also packs some heavy shopping credentials, especially for fashion, accessories and interiors.

Traditional Goods and Souvenirs

If you only had time to visit one shop to pick up a souvenir, then it would have to be **Oriental Bazaar** (page 32) across from Omotesando Hills. The three floors here have everything from fine kimono and antique furniture to cheap and cheerful T-shirts and quirky goods like *sushi*-shaped erasers. The stalls along **Nakamise-dori** in front of **Senso-ji Temple** (page 9) in **Asakusa**, though often a bit too touristy, can also throw up some interesting finds, particularly *yukata* (cotton robes) and traditional snacks such as *senbei* (toasted rice crackers) and *manju* (soft cake with a red bean paste filling). Walk west from Senso-ji, headed toward Ueno, and in about 10 minutes you'll come to the wonderful

Kappabashi-dori, Tokyo's wholesale shopping district for the restaurant industry. The 170 or so shops here deal in nigh on every piece of restaurant equipment and kitchen implement imaginable, including some that specialize in the plastic mock-ups of dishes you'll see in restaurant windows all over town and the paper lanterns that hang outside them. Both make great souvenirs.

Markets

The **Tsukiji fish market** (page 11) and **Ameya Yokocho** street market in Ueno (page 30) are two lively spots that have been covered in detail elsewhere in this book, and both are well worth a visit whether shopping is your thing or not. In addition, Tokyo has plenty of good flea markets and antique markets, including the fantastic **Oedo Antique Market** (antique-market.jp) that's held at Tokyo International Forum in Yurakucho on the first and third Sunday of every month (check the website, as sometimes it's held in Yoyogi, too). The event is Japan's largest outdoor antique market and brings together a good range of fine antiques, curios and bric-a-brac. For a chilled-out afternoon, another good market is the **UNU Farmer's Market** (farmersmarkets.jp), held at the United Nation's University in Omotesando every Saturday and Sunday. As well as organic produce and artisanal farm products, UNU is a good place for handicrafts and also attracts several dozen great food and drink stalls.

Electronics

You will find big home electronics stores like Biku Camera and Yodobashi around most of the major stations in Tokyo, but if you want to dive deep into some electronics and tech shopping, then you will want to head to **Akihabara** on Tokyo's east side. The area picked up its tag as Tokyo's "electric town" with the black market trading of radio parts after World War II and it has since become Japan's undisputed home electronics capital, with giant department stores such as Laox, Yodobashi and Ishimaru Denki retailing everything from the latest cameras and kitchen appliances to massage chairs. Alongside the big players, smaller stores do a roaring trade in specialized electronics parts, robots, used computers and many other electrical items. And adding a different dimension, Akihabara is also known for its *otaku* (geek) shops, in particular those catering to *anime* (animation) and *manga* (comic book) fans. Take a look at page 28 in Chapter 2 for more about the area and its shops.

KYOTO

Kyoto, like Tokyo, offers all sorts of shopping options, from electronics and fashion to arts and crafts. The main shopping area, centered on **Shijo-dori** (page 47), mixes giant **department stores** like Takashimaya, Daimaru and OIOI Marui with small Kyoto specialty food and craft stores and high-end brand names such as

Louis Vuitton. Nearby is **Nishiki-koji Market** (page 47), Kyoto's main food market since the 17th century. It's a mouth-watering riot of color and aromas that stretches for several blocks along a single narrow street.

You'll also find numerous modern stores in and around **JR Kyoto Station**. Among the standouts are an **Isetan** department store and **"The Cube" shopping center** connected to the station building, as well as the sprawling **Porta underground shopping mall**. The real charm of shopping in a historic city like Kyoto, however, are the traditional shopping options. Spend a while roaming Porta and you'll come across a good selection of **craft and souvenir stores** selling items like fans and dolls, sweets and tea. Head to **Kiyomizu Temple** (page 18), and the streets that lead up to the main compound are also a great place for finding handicrafts, in particular Kiyomizu-yaki ceramics. Better yet, and perfect if you get hit by a rainy day that puts a dampener on temple hopping, try the **Kyoto Handicraft Center** (kyotohandicraftcenter.com) near Heian Shrine.

Nishiki Market in Kyoto

It's a one-stop shop that takes in all of Kyoto's fine and wonderful crafts, with items ranging from *kyo-shikki* lacquerware and *ukiyo-e* woodblock prints to *kyo-sensu* folding fans, *kyo-ningyo* dolls and much more. Need a Kabuki Face Pack, boutique coffee maker, kitchen goods for Japanese cuisine? Try **Tokyu Hands** department store on the south side of Shijo-dori, just one block east of Karasuma-dori. The four floors of really imaginative goods make great souvenirs. It's hard to walk out without buying something you did not know you needed before going there.

Several stores known collectively as **Sou Sou** (sousou.co.jp/me) offer some of Japan's trendiest and visionary fashions, with international sizes available. Lots of "size-less" items incorporating Japanese motifs and beautiful workmanship are available, including *tabi* shoes and socks. Shops are located along narrow Kayukoji-dori, which is one block north of Shijo and east of Teramachi-dori.

Antiques

Some of the best stops for antiques can be found on Furumonzen and Shinmonzen streets a little south and east of Sanjo Keihan Station. Both streets extend from Yamata-oji to Higashioji-dori. There is plenty to see and buy, much of it affordable unless one is interested in museum quality items which, understandably, come with a higher price tag. North from Shijo-dori to the Sanjo Keihan Station along Yamata-oji are a number of attractive shops selling textiles, ceramics and prints.

The **Handicraft Center** east of Higashi-oji-dori on the north side of Marutamachi still fulfills the needs of many, whether it is for pearls, woodblock prints, T-shirts, *yukata* robes or antiques. Open 10 a.m. to 6 p.m. Tel: 075-761-8001. japanvisitor.com; kyoto-handicraft-center

The locals' favorite haunt for buying old things (and this includes a huge range of goods from old iron handles to silk-clad dolls or bonsai plants), entails heading to the temple markets in **Toji Temple** on the 21st and to **Kitano-Tenmangu** on the 25th of each month. On the 15th, hand-crafted items are sold at **Chion-ji** on the northeast corner of Imadegawa and Higashi-oji.

On the first Sunday of every month, a small antiques market is held on the grounds of **Toji Temple**. Take a pencil and a piece of paper to overcome the language gap, just write down what you want to pay for an item and see if you get a response. Everyone loves a bargain, and as long as the haggling is friendly both sides can expect to enjoy the encounter. Some vendors will drop prices quickly, especially as the day lengthens. Treasures await the sharp-eyed shopper.

The monthly flea market at Toji Temple in Kyoto

Useful Shopping Phrases

How much is (this)? *(Kore) wa ikura desu ka?*
Do you accept credit cards? *Kurejitto kaado wa tsukaemasu ka?*
It's too expensive: *Taka sugimasu.*
I'll take this: *Kore o kudasai.*
Do you have…? *… wa arimasu ka?*
Cash: *Genkin*

JAPAN'S BEST OUTDOOR ACTIVITIES

Work up a sweat in Japan's breathtakingly beautiful outdoors

Whether you want to raft through foaming rapids, dive alongside schools of tropical fish, ski perfect powder snow or just swing a golf club, Japan's expansive and beautiful outdoors provide a range of great activities. Here is the lowdown of some of the country's most popular outdoor pursuits.

Adventure Sports

Adrenalin junkies rejoice. Japan has got your fix covered. From Tokyo, a great adventure option is to hop on a train two hours north to the hot spring town of **Minakami** in Gunma Prefecture, which in recent years has become something of an adventure sport Mecca. There are companies here offering everything from **trekking** to **rock climbing** and **paragliding** to **whitewater rafting** (there are a dozen or so companies offering rafting alone, including the Kiwi-run canyons.jp). If you are traveling to Shikoku for the Awa-Odori in Tokushima (page 113) or simply passing through Takamatsu (page 64), another great option is to head inland for a couple of days at the picturesque **Oboke Gorge**, where the activities include **whitewater rafting** and **canyoning** (see the Australian-run happyraft.com).

For more on adventure sports in Minakami, see tourism-minakami.com. For elsewhere in Japan, check out the excellent outdoorjapan.com.

Cycling

Many guesthouses now offer bicycles for use by their guests. It is a fabulous way to enjoy places off the main tourist areas. Tiny potted plants in front of homes, small neighborhood restaurants, shops selling handicrafts, this is the next best way to see a city besides on foot. Bicycle rentals have bloomed as well as bicycle sharing spots. Then there are those sites that offer cycling tours in different areas of the country. Among these are spice-roads.com/destination/japan; cycling-japan.jp/ japanbiking.com/

Diving

Diving holidays are big business in Japan, with many Japanese flying off to Guam, Saipan, Hawaii and other exotic destinations on scuba package tours. Back home, the options are pretty good as well, especially if you head to the **Okinawan Islands** (page 71) in the far south. Closer to Tokyo, there are also good dive spots in the **Izu Islands** and off of the **Izu Peninsula**. To find out more about where to dive and how to go about it, divejapan.com is a good starting point.

Golf

In Japan's economic bubble era, no pastime said "wealth" quite like golf. Club memberships cost a small fortune, making a regular round impossible for anyone without a corporate membership, generous expense account or hefty income. Driving ranges were as close as many golfers got to playing the game. Things, however, have changed considerably as a result of the country's lingering economic malaise. Although Japan still has its prestigious members-only clubs, the majority of the country's 2,500 or so courses are now open to non-members and many offer very

Hiking in Kirigamine Heights, Nagano

affordable rates, especially on weekdays. A round at the cheapest of public courses in Greater Tokyo, although rather plain, can cost as little as ¥5,000. Many decent, challenging courses cost under ¥10,000 mid-week. As for the golfing experience and etiquette in Japan, it doesn't vary much from golf elsewhere in the world, with perhaps the odd exception that most groups stop for lunch after only playing the front nine (you can forget about a swift 18 holes) and clothing is always formal. To find out more and locate an English-friendly course or driving range, check out Outdoor Japan's excellent website, golf-in-japan.com

Hiking

From treks that would challenge the most experienced hikers to simple jaunts from Tokyo, Japan has something for everyone. That's probably not surprising considering that more than 70% of the country is mountainous. If you wanted to do some serious hiking, then head to Japan's premier hiking grounds, the northern part of the **Japan Alps**, typically accessed via the town of **Kamikochi** (kamikochi.org/category/national-park/) in Nagano Prefecture. At an elevation of 1,500 meters (4,900 feet), the air is crystal clear as are the shallow rivers that course the park, allowing visitors to gaze at wondrous multi-colored fish that inhabit the river.

In addition to hiking, day visitors enjoy walking the raised trails, and birders find **Kamikochi** a true paradise. Visitor numbers are restricted and cars are no longer allowed, but parking facilities are available a few kilometers away with a frequent shuttle bus service. The area is closed during winter months and hotel reservations open on April 1. The best way to get here is by JR train from Takayama or Matsumoto or by joining a bus tour for an overnight stay.

Another mountainous location to visit is **Nakasendo**. In the midst of towering mountains, slim pathways lead to the simple dwellings of the post town inhabitants. Fishing, woodcutting, hunting and farming were their world and the steep terrain made building on higher slopes impractical and distances to necessities for survival great. The houses hug the narrow roadway—structures with dark wooden lattice frontage and adjoining walls built on slanting ground reveal a purity of design that makes two of the Nakasendo route—Tsumago and Magome—particularly charming and picturesque. The walk between the two towns at a leisurely pace takes about two hours. The closest JR station from Tokyo is Nagiso and from Kyoto, Nakatsugawa. Local buses go infrequently to both towns. Bus timetables can be found at japanguide.com/e/e2015.html

You can also get in a good range of day hikes (or longer) from Tokyo by heading west to the **Okutama** and **Tanzawa** areas. The simplest trip of all, a hike up the 599-meter (1,965-foot) **Mount Takao** (takaotozan.co.jp), starts just a 50-minute train ride west of Shinjuku and even includes the option of taking a cable car more than half way to the summit. For a brief taste of the mountains, some welcome fresh air and good views across to Mount Fuji (page 14), it's a really worthwhile trip. You can add a couple more nearby peaks to it, to get away from the crowds and make a very full day out.

For information on hiking trails, advice on when to go and what to take, and plenty of other useful info, check out outdoorjapan.com. If you are keen to get a lot of hiking in while in Japan, the *Lonely Planet*'s hiking guide for Japan is hard to beat; it's led us on many a good jaunt.

Skiing and Snowboarding

With the perfect powder snow and prime ski grounds of **Niseko** in **Hokkaido**, Japan's skiing and boarding scene can rival anywhere in the world. Niseko is so good that the area is covered in detail in Japan's "Don't Miss" Sights, page 25. But if getting to Hokkaido isn't possible, don't worry. Japan has an embarrassment of winter riches, so much so you don't actually have to go far from Tokyo for good snow. About 80 minutes from Tokyo Station via the *shinkansen*, the town of **Echigo Yuzawa** is a really good option, with several well-developed ski and snowboarding fields around the town that offer everything from night skiing to

kids slopes and several-kilometer long runs for advanced skiers and boarders. And like Niseko, Echigo Yuzawa (especially at the Gala Ski Resort) is well geared to English speaking as well as Japanese-speaking visitors.

For more on Niseko and Yuzawa, as well as many other skiing and snowboarding areas across Japan, see Snow Japan (skijapanguide.com).

The ski resorts in **Nagano Prefecture** are some of Japan's steepest and best equipped as are the region's hot springs. After the 1998 Nagano Olympics, the amenities got even better and Nagano became a year-round resort. Besides the skiing facilities of Hakuba, Tsugaike, Happo, Norikura and Akakura these towns along this JR train route offer summer visitors a needed escape from the languid humidity in coastal cities. While walking the trails, one will meet hikers, photography clubs, families on outings, picnickers, and enthusiasts after the elusive beetle and butterfly. The hills are truly alive.

The best way to get to this area is via JR trains from Nagoya, Nakano and Matsumoto.

Niseko Ski Resort in Hokkaido

JAPAN'S PARKS AND GARDENS

Oases of beauty and calm

Heavily influenced by the seasons, full of subtleties and rich in symbolism, Japan's gardens are canvases upon which the country's garden designers reflect the nation's soul. There's something calming yet stimulating about a walk through a traditional stroll garden, while the enigmatic nature of certain Zen gardens can be both meditative and baffling. Several of Japanese finest gardens, such as the dry landscape garden at **Ryoan-ji Temple** (page 50) in Kyoto and the nearby **Daitoku-ji** (page 51), are covered in full in Chapter Two. Below is a selection of even more truly magnificent parks and gardens.

Tokyo Stroll Gardens

Tokyo has a lovely selection of classic stroll gardens. **Rikugi-en** near Ikebukuro, a garden built in the 15th century and inspired by *waka* poetry, is especially charming in autumn when the foliage turns to red and rust. You also have the pristine landscapes of **Koishikawa Koraku-en**, where the "borrowed scenery" (a common feature of classic gardens) nowadays includes part of Tokyo Dome next door. The iris garden at **Meiji Jingu shrine** (most beautiful in June), **Hama-Rikyu Garden** near Shiodome and **Chinzan-so** in Bunkyo Ward all deserve a shout-out, too. But of all Tokyo's traditional gardens, it's always been **Kiyosumi Teien** that has done it for me, in small part because it's my local garden and I've napped away many a sunny afternoon there. But mostly it's because no matter how often I visit, it's always beautiful and always calming. Centered on a large pond with islets at its heart and landscaped pathways encircling it, the garden once belonged to the founder of Mitsubishi, Iwasaki Yataro, who used it as a place for his employees to relax and to entertain visiting dignitaries. Today, it's a public park that attracts all sorts, from brides and grooms posing for wedding photos to elderly art groups who come to paint the traditional teahouse reflected in its carp-filled waters.

A short walk from Kiyosumi-Shirakawa Station on the Oedo and Hanzomon subway lines. teien.tokyo-park.or.jp/en/kiyosumi

Shinjuku Gyoen Park, Tokyo

Like many of Japan's finest parks and gardens, **Shinjuku Gyoen** has a long history dating back to the Edo era when it was part of a *daimyo*'s residence, and then becoming an imperial garden dur-

Hama-Rikyu Garden in Tokyo

Okochi Sanso Villa in Kyoto

ing the Meiji period before opening to the public shortly after World War II. Over those years it has developed into a wonderful mish-mash of garden styles, its 140 acres (57 hectares) combining formal French garden designs, traditional Japanese elements, English landscaping and a greenhouse complex, home to 2,400 tropical and subtropical species. Altogether there are some 20,000 trees across the grounds, ranging from Himalayan cedars and bald cypresses to the cherry blossoms that make the park's central sprawling lawn a stunning *hanami* spot in late March and early April. Strolling the peaceful grounds, it's hard to imagine you are within walking distance of one of the world's busiest train stations and a stone's throw from the busy streets of Shinjuku (page 33).

A 10-minute walk from Shinjuku Station or a 5-minute walk from either Shinjuku-gyoen-mae Station (Marunouchi Line) or Shinjuku 3-chome Station (Toei Shinjuku Line). env.go.jp/garden/shinjukugyoen

Okochi Sanso Villa, Kyoto

The approach to the former villa of one of Japan's beloved actors, Denjiro Okochi, is reached by walking through a path of towering bamboo, the leaves forming a green canopy meters overhead, unlike anywhere else in Japan. The 10-minute stroll ends at the entrance of **Okochi Sanso**, the park-size grounds which

include a view of the Western Mountains and the city, a former movie star's estate, a tearoom, a middle gate and a small Buddhist shrine where Okochi used to meditate, all structures designated as Tangible Cultural Properties. The gardens are extensive, with many unique roof-tile inlaid pathways and a huge selection of carefully chosen stepping stones. The northern vista is of Mount Hiei and the Hozu River gorge backed by a steep mountainside, the colors providing a luscious seasonal palette throughout the hilly landscape. Fee of ¥1,000, ¥500 for H.S. students includes a bowl of whipped green tea and a sweet.

A 15-min. walk from the JR, Keifuku and Hankyu train lines. Open 9 a.m. to 5 p.m.

Ritsurin Garden, Takamatsu

Started in the 1600s and taking more than 100 years to complete, Takamatsu's (page 64) main attraction is an epic affair. Spread over 185 acres (75 hectares), the garden blends six carp-filled ponds, a dozen or so man-made hills, numerous ornate bridges, a dazzling array of flora and fauna and borrowed scenery that includes the pine-covered Mount Shiun to create a truly mesmerizing experience. At each turn you are met with a new landscape, typically accented by seasonal colors like the gentle pinks of cherry blossoms in spring, the varied colored hydrangeas in June or the warming red leaves of the park's maples in November. Add to that, when you have finished walking you can stop for a bowl of *matcha* (green tea) at one of the Edo-era teahouses that merge perfectly with the landscaped surroundings.

A 3-minute walk from JR Ritsurin Koen Kitaguchi Station, which is one stop from JR Takamatsu Station, or a 10-minute taxi ride from JR Takamatsu. pref.kagawa.lg. jp/ritsurin

Tofuku-ji Temple, Kyoto

To describe anything as a "hidden gem" is a cliché so frowned upon in travel writing circles that I might have to consider a career change. But that's exactly what the gardens at Tofuku-ji are. Despite being just one station south of Kyoto Station, and with that far more accessible than most of Kyoto's main draws, it's entirely possible to take in the gardens and barely see another soul. Maybe Tofuku-ji's gardens don't get the crowds of Ryoan-ji or Kinkaku-ji because, though rich in traditional Zen conceptualism, they are by Kyoto standards a modern affair. They were built in 1939 by landscape gardener Mirei Shigemori, who arranged them in quarters around the temple's main hall (the Hojo), in the process adding subtle modern accents to the traditional designs. The southern garden, set in front of the main hall, features groupings of rocks and mossy "mountains" on a

raked sand base to create a Zen archipelago. The northern garden is like a checkers board of moss and paving tiles. The eastern garden uses cylindrical stones arranged on a lush mossy carpet to depict the Ursa Major (Great Bear) constellation. And the western garden has trimmed azalea shrubs dividing squares of moss and sand in the Chinese *seiden* style. Each of the gardens is worth a visit in its own right. Together they are stunning.

An 8-minute walk from Tofukiji Station on the Nara Line, one stop south of Kyoto Station. tofukiji.jp

"Three Great Gardens" of Japan

Aside from **Kenroku-en** ("garden with six characteristics," mentioned on page 43) in Kanazawa, there are two other gardens that form the Nihon Sanemei-en (the Three Great Gardens of Japan). Kenroku-en is unique in that it incorporates all six traditional qualities to which Japanese gardens are said to aspire—spaciousness and seclusion, artifice and antiquity, watercourses and panoramas—all the while reflecting the four seasons, from the plum and cherry blossoms in spring through to snow-capped pines and stone lanterns in winter. **Koraku-en**, set across the moat from Okayama Castle, is designed in the *kaiyu* style, wherein at every twist and turn of the pathway the visitor is presented with a change of scenery. The final member of the three, **Kairaku-en** in Mito, Ibaraki, is at its best in early spring when its several thousand plum blossom trees paint the grounds an incredible panorama of white, pink and red.

A 6-minute walk from Okayama Station and a 1.5-hour journey from Kyoto on the Tokaido-Sanyo Shinkansen. Kairaku-en is a 2-hour train ride from Tokyo Station. Board the train at Mito Station.

Tofuku-ji garden

KID-FRIENDLY ATTRACTIONS

The perfect antidote after one too many temples

Tokyo Disney Resort

Tokyo Disney Resort

Ever since the "Magic Kingdom" came to Japan in 1983, it's had the country under a spell that Cinderella's fairy godmother would be proud of. The resort, which includes the separate Disneyland and more adult-friendly DisneySea, attracts 14 million visitors annually, making it the third most-visited theme park in the world. The visitors flock in for Disney's trademark colorful parades and big production stage shows, its mix of white-knuckle rides and fun activities, and plenty of other attractions featuring well-known Disney characters. The only issue, bar the crowds, is convincing the kids to leave. To avoid the first of those problems, make sure you go on a weekday outside of the school holidays.

Accessed via Tokyo Station to Maihama on the Keiyo Line or by express bus from Shinjuku. tokyodisneyresort.co.jp

Museum of Emerging Science and Innovation, Tokyo

The idea of visiting a museum might not appeal to some kids but a trip to the Miraikan (as it's familiarly known) will change that forever. Designed to cater to kids of all ages and all attention spans, the five floors of this high-tech museum are packed with hands-on educational exhibits covering everything from the International Space Station and extreme environments to life sciences and the human brain. All of them—and this is still something of a rarity in Japan—come with perfect English language explanations. Before you go, make sure to check the equally well prepared website so you can time your visit with one of the museum's regular demonstrations of cutting-edge tech. Recent ones have included ASIMO humanoid robots and futuristic electricity-powered unicycles.

A 5-minute walk from the Fune-no-Kagakukan or Telecom Center stations on the Yurikamome Line. miraikan.jst.go.jp/en

Joypolis, Tokyo

There are plenty of "game centers" in Tokyo, some accidentally retro and smoky, others with modern games, but none come close to Sega's three-story Joypolis indoor amusement park in Odaiba. The virtual-reality games here will blow the minds of the most battle-hardened Play Station 3 addicts, be it the hang-glider simulator or half-pipe machine. And if they don't, even money says the slick car racing cabinets or ear-splitting shoot-em-ups will.

A few minutes walk from Odaiba-kaihinkoen Station on the Yurikamome Line. tokyo-joypolis.com

Sanrio Puroland, Tokyo

Let's get one thing straight about Sanrio Puroland: the super cute home of Hello Kitty is aimed at kids, yet thanks to

Sagano Scenic Railway, Kyoto

Iwatayama Monkey Park, Kyoto

Japan's fondness for *kawaii* (cuteness) also has a worryingly loyal adult following. If you have kids obsessed by things pink and sparkly, Puroland's mix of Hello Kitty musical revues and dance shows won't disappoint. Neither for that matter will the small selection of equally kitsch rides and shops.

The nearest station is Tama Center Station, 40 minutes from Shinjuku on the Keio Line. puroland.co.jp

Hanayashiki Amusement Park, Tokyo

Some would call Hanayashiki in Asakusa decrepit, others charmingly retro. As the oldest amusement park in the country, Hanayashiki's 20 or so old-fashioned attractions are ideal for younger kids yet to have been wooed by the far more fanciful offerings of Disney or Universal Studios. The park's traditional merry-go-round is a timeless attraction, the rickety haunted house is surprisingly eerie and the two-seater helicopters that you can pedal on rails high above the park offer unexpectedly good views of Senso-ji Temple and Tokyo Sky Tree. Best of all is the roller coaster, which, dating to 1953 is Japan's oldest. It could well be the country's least terrifying, too, given that it trundles its way around the park at an almost genteel 40 km/h (25 miles/h).

A 5-minute walk from Asakusa Station on the Ginza, Toei Asakusa and Tobu Isesaki lines. hanayashiki.net

Sakuda Gold and Silver Leaf, Tokyo

The showroom and workshop are not just for children although they will learn a great deal about gold from just seeing the exhibits. One must book in advance for a hands-on experience.

Open 9 a.m. to 5.30 p.m. Admission ¥600; children ¥250. goldleaf-sakuda.jp/

Sagano Scenic Railway (Torokko Train)

Japanese love their trains, so when a newer, faster route was laid in 1989 these older tracks were preserved. The line was started up again with an outfitted retro-looking train that has one open car, the others with windows for when the weather turns chilly. The Hozugawa River that slices through the western mountains is renowned for its steep hillsides and glorious seasonal color, and the 25-minute ride to Kameoka Station offers a spectacular look at the heavily wooded mountainside and river below.

A 5-minute walk from JR Sagano Station, ¥620 one-way. A return trip on the regular JR Sagano line is ¥200 and takes 7 minutes, or continue on to Kyoto Station for ¥320, which takes 15 minutes. Closed Wednesday and from December 30 to the end of February.

Iwatayama Monkey Park, Kyoto

Japan hosts the most northern-dwelling monkeys in the world, the Japanese macaque. These monkeys are native to

Universal Studios, Osaka

Osaka Aquarium

all the islands except Hokkaido, and although wild, are studied and tracked by Kyoto University Primate Institute. The walk up the 160-meter (525-feet) hill is steep but signs along the way give interesting facts about its inhabitants (in Japanese). Once on top, there is a small hut in which peanuts are sold for ¥100 for visitors to feed the monkeys who scamper and climb the fence that separates you from them. One word of advice, don't feed the cute little ones first or you are likely to see the older monkeys swatting them away as they swipe that peanut from the young one, and don't stare at the adult males as it is a sign of aggression. People are inside; the monkeys are outside, so you can feed them while enjoying being as close to a wild creature as possible. One word of advice, never feed them outside or you will have an encounter that you may regret. Feeding times mean the staff will scatter soybeans, another moment to watch the antics outside.

A 5-minute walk from Hankyu Railways, 15 minutes from Keifuku Rail and 20 minutes from JR rail. ¥500; children ¥250. Open 9 a.m. to 4.30 p.m. in winter, 5.30 p.m. in summer.monkeypark.jp/

Universal Studios Japan, Osaka

When it opened in 2001 as Universal's first theme park in Asia, USJ was heralded as Kansai's answer to the Magic Kingdom. More than 17 years on, with 8 million people coming through the door annually, it's the only theme park in Japan that comes anywhere near the visitor numbers Tokyo Disney Resort keeps pulling in. And for a very good reason. It's brilliant. Packed with simulators, white-knuckle rides and kid friendly attractions based on movies like *Back to the Future, Terminator 2, Spiderman, Shrek, ET* and many others, USJ manages to cater not just to kids but also to adults. It's a great family day out.

Accessed via Universal City Station on the JR Yumesaki Line. usj.co.jp/e

Osaka Aquarium

With 27 tanks holding a total of 10,941 tons of water, the Osaka Aquarium (Kaiyukan) is one of the largest public aquariums in the world, its exhibits documenting the varied habitats found across the Pacific Ocean's entire "Ring of Fire." There are areas dedicated to sea otters and giant salamander, others to spotted seals, Californian sea lions and numerous other species living in the Ring. The largest tank of the lot, which is 9 meters (30 feet) deep and holds 5,400 cubic meters (190,700 cubic feet) of water, brings together whale sharks, manta rays, bluefin tuna and other fish, with spectacular effect.

A 5-minute walk from Osaka-ko Station on the Chuo subway line. kaiyukan.com

JAPAN'S BEST GALLERIES AND MUSEUMS

Soak up modern art and classic culture

Be they specializing in cutting-edge modern art, classic Japanese crafts or European Masters, Japan has some of the very best museums and galleries in the world. In Tokyo, Ueno alone has enough museums to keep culture vultures occupied for a couple of days (see Chapter 2, page 30 for a rundown on those), while contemporary art hounds could spend days exploring central and western Tokyo and barely scratch the surface of the city's vibrant art and museum scene. Here's the lowdown on the best of those and many more top galleries and museums across Japan.

TOKYO AREA

National Art Center

The National Art Center in Roppongi rightly describes itself as unique and innovative. First, the ultramodern building is on an unprecedented scale for an art facility in Japan, comprising 14,000 square meters (151,000 square feet) of exhibition space. Second, despite its size, and unlike its sister museums the National Museum of Modern Art in Kyoto and the National Museum of Modern Art in Tokyo, it doesn't have a permanent collection but instead puts on a variety of exhibitions each year, ranging from Impressionism and retrospectives of Chinese contemporary art.
A 5-minute walk from Roppongi Station on the Oedo and Hibiya subway lines. nact.jp/english

Mori Art Museum

Located on the 53rd floor of the sleek Roppongi Hills urban development (page 10), the Mori Art Museum's two spacious exhibition spaces attract works from a

The National Art Center in Roppongi

Mori Art Museum

dazzling array of top international and Japanese contemporary artists, previous shows having included a Turner Prize retrospective and exhibitions on contemporary Japanese architecture. Most recently, as part of the museum's 15th anniversary celebrations in 2018, the highlights included a major "Japan in Architecture" exhibition tracing the evolution of architecture and architects from ancient times until the present. *Located in Roppongi Hills, a several-minute walk from Roppongi Station on the Oedo and Hibiya subway lines. mori.art.museum*

Design Festa Gallery

This old apartment block turned gallery in the back streets of Harajuku (page 32) is the heartbeat of Tokyo's freestyle art scene. The numerous small exhibition spaces here offer up an ever-changing line-up of art from up-and-coming artists that covers an incredible range of artistic expression, from painting and performance art to photography and sculpture. In between the exhibition rooms, there's color everywhere. The hallways and walls of DF's laid-back café and *okonomiyaki* restaurant are covered in murals and graffiti, and even the trash cans and drink machines have been blitzed with art. It's youthful, fun and refreshing.

A 5-minute walk from Meijijingumae subway station or a 10-minute walk from JR Harajuku Station. designfestagallery. com

Nezu Museum

This Omotesando (page 32) museum houses industrialist Kaichiro Nezu's (1860–1940) magnificent collection of Japanese and other pre-modern Asian art, the 7,400 pieces of which include seven items designated as National Treasures and some 200 others registered as Important Cultural Properties or Important Art Objects. Among the many highlights within Nezu's former residence, which was augmented in 2009 by a strikingly modern Kuma Kengo-designed building, keep an eye out for the folding screen painting "Irises" by the 17th-century artist Ogata Korin and the museum's collection of ancient Chinese bronzes. After that, pop outside for a walk around the teahouse-dotted garden and its ponds, which offer up the kind of space and calm you wouldn't think possible (or affordable for anyone but a tycoon) in Omotesando. *An 8-minute walk from exit A5 of Omotesando Station on the Ginza, Hanzomon and Chiyoda subway lines. nezu-muse.or.jp*

Hakone Open Air Museum

When the Hakone Open Air Museum opened in 1969 it was the first open-air art museum in Japan. With more than 120 works displayed on its 70,000 square meters (753,2000 square feet) of scenic grounds, plus five exhibition halls that include a pavilion home to more than 300 Picassos, it's still the best museum of its kind. The outdoor exhibits include works from internationally acclaimed sculptors such as Bourdelle, Rodin, Miro and Moore. In fact, the OAM has the world's largest Henry Moore collection with 26 pieces on a rotated exhibition schedule. Adding a welcome and soothing quirk to a visit, the museum also has an outdoor foot-bath spa where you can stop and soak your feet in natural hot spring water. It's the perfect way to end a day of exploring wonderful artworks in fittingly beautiful surroundings. *hakone-oam.or.jp*

Ishikawa Prefectural Museum of Traditional Arts and Crafts

The two-story museum offers fine displays of local work accompanied by videos showing the artisans producing their craft. The tiny shop on the first floor has a tempting array of beautiful goods. *shofu.pref.ishikawa.jp/densankan/*

21st Century Museum of Contemporary Art

Outside of the garden and castle grounds is perhaps one of Kanazawa's most extraordinary example of a modern museum, one that is completely round in design. Exhibits change throughout the year, but Erlich's "Swimming Pool" and Turrell's "Blue Planet Sky" are favorites. *kanazawa21.jp*

KYOTO

Kyoto has a good mix of museums and galleries, covering everything from traditional craft to contemporary art. Three very good ones, the **National Museum of Modern Art** (momak.go.jp), the **Hosomi Museum** (emuseum.or.jp) and the **Kyoto Municipal Museum of Art** (city.kyoto.jp/bunshi/kmma) are covered in Chapter 2, page 49. On top of those, the **Kyoto National Museum** (kyohaku.go.jp) often puts on worthwhile special exhibitions that in recent years have included the calligraphy of Japanese emperors and Heian court culture. The **Kyoto Museum of Traditional Crafts** (miyakomesse.jp/fureaika), near Heian Shrine, does a great job of documenting the diversity and quality of Japan's traditional crafts, covering everything from ceramics to kimono making. Also in the Heian Shrine area, the **Kyoto Handicraft Center** (kyotohandicraftcenter.com) doubles as a gallery and store, with seven floors of beautiful produce, hands-on workshops and demonstrations by local artisans.

Kiyomizu Sannenzaka Museum (sannenzaka-museum.co.jp) is a newcomer with exquisitely crafted items of cloisonné and lacquerware from late Edo. Another little gem is the old samurai warrior's home turned into a **Netsuke Museum** (netsuke.jp/en) filled with the miniature ivory carvings that Japanese carried attached as toggles on their tobacco pouches. The glass-encased exhibits in the *tatami* rooms offer a unique look into ancient Japanese design motifs.

Miho Museum

This I.M.Pei architectural work of art is located in neighboring Shiga Prefecture, a 90-minute train and bus ride from Kyoto. Opened in 1997, 80% of this extraordinary structure was built underground so that natural light can illuminate the exhibits. The main building is approached through a tunnel and bridge, allowing the visitor to leave behind the mundane and enter the enlightened world of art. The collection ranges from Japanese tea utensils to Buddhist masterpieces of sculpture as well as Egyptian and Iranian objects. Interior gardens are masterful examples of landscaping. The two cafés offer simple refreshment in spectacular settings. Open 10 a.m. to 5 p.m. Closed on Monday. Closed from mid-December to mid-March. Admission: adults ¥1,100. *miho.jp/*

Lake Biwa Museum

Four million years ago, this volcano erupted and eventually formed Biwa Ko, Japan's largest lake. Built on the lakeside in Shiga Prefecture, the museum has displays of its geological beginnings, early settlements, underwater archeological work and a large aquarium. Videos show lifestyles from other large lakes in the world. There are touch tanks and docents to assist and answer questions. Great for children and adults alike. The café overlooks the lakeside and its landscaped paths. Open 9.30 a.m. to 5 p.m. Tel: 077-568-4811. Closed Mondays unless Monday is a national holiday after which it closes on Tuesday. Check for irregular closings. Admission ¥750; Univ. H.S. students; ¥400; Jr. H.S and under, free *lbm.go.jp/english/index.html*

OSAKA

Osaka more than holds its own on the museum front, with standouts including the well-presented and kid-friendly **Osaka History Museum** (mus-his.city.osaka.jp), which documents Osaka's development from pre-feudal days to the present, and the **Municipal Museum of Fine Art** (osaka-art-museum.jp) and its vast collection of lacquerware, 12th- to 14th-century Japanese art, woodblock prints and much more. Osaka does well when it comes to crafts too. The **Museum of Oriental Ceramics** (moco.or.jp), which is situated in Osaka's Nakano-shima Park, boasts an internationally acclaimed collection of antique Chinese, Korean and Japanese ceramics, while the **Nihon Mingei-kan** in Senri Expo Park brings together handicrafts from Okinawa, Hokkaido and everywhere in between.

NAOSHIMA
Benesse House Museum

The Tadao Ando-designed Benesse House gallery and hotel (page 83) started Naoshima's transformation from ailing fishing community to thriving arty island when it opened in 1992. It's still Naoshima's artistic highlight, with 20 or so outdoor art installations from artists such as Kusama Yayoi, Walter De Maria and Cai Guo-Qiang dotted about its tranquil beachfront and clifftop grounds. That would be impressive enough, but

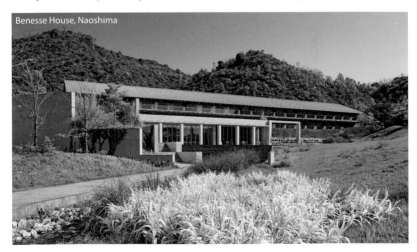
Benesse House, Naoshima

add an indoor collection that includes works by Hockney, Warhol and a host of exciting contemporary Japanese artists, not to mention one of Japan's hippest hotels, and Benesse House is simply stunning. *benesse-artsite.jp/en/ benessehouse*

Chichu Art Museum
Opened in 2004, Chichu Art Museum is another of Tadao Ando's masterful Naoshima creations. The structure, which is built into a hillside and utilizes mostly natural light to illuminate its cavernous concrete interior, is home to a collection that runs from Monet paintings through to modern masters James Turrell and Walter De Maria, whose grandiose installations and site-specific works blend perfectly with Ando's sleek architecture. *benesse-artsite.jp/en/chichu*

Art House Project
Since 1998, the Art House Project in Honmura village has seen seven of the village's traditional structures turned into permanent art installations. It all began when artist Tatsuo Miyajima restored a 200-year-old house with the help of villagers and then installed an abstract mix of water features and LED and digital displays. Other artists then followed suit, restoring buildings and reinventing their interiors, creating a collection of installations and small galleries that blend effortlessly into what is still a charming old village. *benesse-artsite.jp/en/ arthouse*

HIROSHIMA
Peace Memorial Museum
In tandem with the Peace Memorial Park (page 22), Hiroshima's Peace Memorial Museum is an incredibly moving testament to the horrors of nuclear armament. The main building displays exhibits designed to highlight the events and immediate aftermath of August 6th, 1945, documenting the horrific impact the blast, heat rays and radiation had on Hiroshima and its people. It's a humbling experience to absorb the harrowing photographs taken after the explosion and to view artifacts that include charred lunch boxes and shredded school uniforms. But there is also a lot of hope on display here, the east building focusing largely on Hiroshima before the bomb and the city's incredible recovery since. *pcf.city.hiroshima.jp*

Hiroshima Peace Memorial Park

FESTIVALS AND EVENTS

Experience Japan's most vibrant and colorful matsuri

From snow festivals to vibrant summer firework displays and historic parades, Japan loves its festivals. The hot summer months, in particular, see a near endless lineup of *matsuri*, big and small, taking place all over the country, but whenever and wherever you travel in Japan the chances are good that you will be able to experience a festival of some kind. If you are really lucky, your trip will coincide with the following events.

WINTER
Sapporo Snow Festival, Hokkaido

Held every February since the 1950s and seemingly growing in scale with each passing year, the Sapporo Snow Festival is Japan's premier winter event. (Visit snowfes.com for the exact dates each year.) Over the course of a week, it attracts some two million people from across Japan and overseas. The crowds come for the hundreds of splendid snow statues and ice sculptures that turn Odori Park, the community dome Tsudome, the main street in Susukino and other parts of central Sapporo (page 67) into a wintery outdoor art gallery. The snow and ice artworks vary from large-scale replicas of world wonders, such as the Pyramids of Giza to simple igloos and kid-built snowmen. In a city that sells itself as a "winter wonderland," Sapporo is never more wonderful.
snowfes.com

SPRING
Cherry Blossom Viewing

From mid-March to early May, a wave of cherry blossom spreads northward across Japan, signaling the advent of spring with an explosion of delicate pink petals. The blossoms send the country into a frenzy, with the major TV channels following the petals' progress and people heading to parks and blossom viewing (*hanami*) spots en masse to picnic and party in the *sakura*'s shade. You can feel the country letting out a collective "ah, spring at last."

Cherry blossom viewing in Ueno Park, Tokyo

Sanja Matsuri, Tokyo

In Tokyo, Ueno Park (page 30) is popular for saké-fueled cherry blossom parties when the petals peak there in early April, while the Chidorigafuchi section of the Imperial Palace's moat (page 35) is the city's most picturesque *hanami* spot. In Kyoto, where the blossoms peak all over the city around the first week of April, the best viewing spots include Maruyama Park behind Yasaka Shrine (page 49) and the Okazaki Canal near Heian Shrine.

Sanja Matsuri, Tokyo

Tokyo has plenty of festivals, but none can beat the high-octane Sanja Matsuri. For three days in mid-May every year, the streets of Asakusa (page 29) explode into life with one of Japan's largest and liveliest parades of *mikoshi* (portable shrines). Hundreds of thousands of onlookers cram onto the streets as teams carry—hollering all the while—the portable shrines on their shoulders. Alongside the *mikoshi*, the festivities include colorful food stalls and parades of floats on which traditional musicians hammer out unrelenting drum beats and flutists weave intoxicating tunes. And it's all played out against a backdrop that takes in some

of Tokyo's most distinctive structures: Senso-ji Temple, Tokyo Sky Tree and the Philippe Starck-designed Asahi Beer Hall. Visit jnto.or.jp for exact dates.

SUMMER
Hyakuman-goku, Kanazawa

On the second Saturday of June, the city begins a three-day festival commemorating the entry of Lord Maeda who established the Kaga clan and built the castle. Participants dressed as samurai in ancient costume parade through its main streets. *Taiko* drumming, lion dances, tea ceremonies, *noh* drama and over 100,000 people dancing in the streets add to the atmosphere. Continuing a 400-year tradition, paper lanterns with lit candles are floated down the Kanazawa River.

Gion Matsuri, Kyoto

The Gion Matsuri, Kyoto's biggest festival, and now an Intangible World Heritage, has unusual roots. It apparently began as a form of prayer to ward off a plague in 869. Today it is an exquisite procession of art-laden floats. In its current form, the festival lasts the entire month

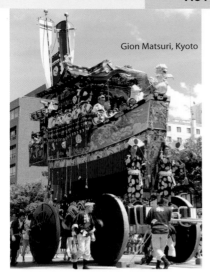
Gion Matsuri, Kyoto

mikoshi (portable shrines). The second, and more spectacular, sees the same 3,000 sail in a procession of decorated boats, which at nightfall have bonfires lit on their decks. If that weren't enough, the event wraps up with a fireworks display that sees 4,000 rockets briefly turn the Osakan sky into a Pollockesque canvas.

Sumidagawa Fireworks, Tokyo

From small local neighborhood shows to extravagant events that bring cities to a near halt, Japan has firework displays going on all over in summer. Illuminating Tokyo's eastern skies on the final Saturday of July, the Sumidagawa Hanabi Taikai is one of the best. With in excess of 20,000 rockets swirling, exploding and painting a rainbow of colors above the Sumida River, the only thing that comes close to the colors in the sky are the vibrant summer *yukata* worn by many in the heaving crowds. If you can't make the Sumidagawa display, other big ones include the Tokyo Bay Fireworks in August (with 12,000 rockets), the display at the Tenjin Matsuri in Osaka (see this page) and the August display above Itsukushima Shrine in Miyajima (page 61). *sumidagawa-hanabi.com*

of July, with its main processions taking place on July 17 and 24th when 16 elaborately decorated floats (33 in total) are manually pulled through central Kyoto carrying musicians and dancers dressed in exquisite traditional attire. During and before the procession days, many parts of the city are pedestrianized, the cars banished so the hundreds of thousands of festival goers can wander the food stalls and amusements leisurely. It's a wonderful time to be in Kyoto, but make sure you book hotels a long, long way in advance.

Tenjin Matsuri, Osaka

Osakans know how to put on a show and the Tenjin Matsuri is one they've been putting on with aplomb for more than 1,000 years. Held every July 24th and 25th and centered on Tenman-gu Shrine (although festivities spread out all over the city), the festival encompasses all sorts of activities, from *bunraku* puppet shows to *kagura* musical performances, but it's Tenjin's two processions that form the centerpiece. The first sees a parade of 3,000 people dressed in imperial court styles from the 8th to 12th centuries marching through the streets alongside

Awa-Odori, Tokushima

None of Shikoku's traditions—and the island is rich with many—has anywhere as near as much unbridled revelry as the Awa-Odori festival of folkdance in Tokushima, which takes place annually from August 12th to 15th. Dating to 1587 and a drunken celebration for the then newly built Tokushima Castle, the Awa-Odori racks up some incredible numbers, with almost 100,000 dancers descending on Tokushima and at least tenfold more spectators packing the city's streets to cheer them on. The dancing itself is characterized by irregular steps and an

Awa-Odori folk dance festival, Tokushima

Grand Autumn Festival, Nikko

up-tempo rhythm, with colorfully dressed male and female troupes dancing through the humid streets of Tokushima to a pulsating musical mix of drums, flutes, gongs and three-stringed *sanshin*. In a single word, you could call it intoxicating. If you make it to Tokushima for the event, don't forget your dancing shoes. As the official dancing merges into after parties and late night free-for-alls, everyone and anyone can take part. To give a rough translation of the Awa-Odori's rallying cry, "you are a fool if you dance and a fool if you don't, so you might as well dance." *awanavi.jp/english*

AUTUMN
Reitaisai, Kamakura

The Reitaisai festival, which is held every year at Tsuruoka Hachiman-gu Shrine in Kamakura (page 38) from September 14th to 16th, is as much a display of skill as it is tradition. As with many festivals, there's classical dancing and parades, food stalls and amusements. There is worship, too. But the undoubted highlight of the event, in fact what has given the event its fame, is the *yabusame* horseback archery contest on the final day. Popular with samurai during the Kamakura period (1192–1333), the contest is a demonstration of both horse-

manship and martial artistry in which riders in samurai hunting gear gallop along a straight stretch of track unleashing clinically accurate arrows en route. All done with the measured poise of a *noh* performance and the deadly skill and speed of a stealth attack, it's breathtaking to watch. *hachimangu.or.jp*

Grand Autumn Festival, Nikko

Visit Nikko's Tosho-gu Shrine (see Japan's "Don't Miss" Sights, page 13) for its aptly named Grand Autumn Festival on October 16th and 17th and you could be forgiven for thinking you've slipped through a time warp back to the Edo era. The climax of the two-day festival sees 800 men dressed as Edo-era samurai proceed in file through the Tosho-gu area behind a single portable shrine in a display of pageantry that is believed to have started as a reproduction of the funeral ceremony of the man who built Tosho-gu and unified Japan to begin the Edo era, shogun Tokugawa Ieyasu. The day before the procession, the festival also includes a skillful display of *yabusame* horseback archery horse, like the Reitaisai festival in Kamakura (see this page). And if you can't make it to Nikko in autumn, don't worry. Try spring. Tosho-gu's Grand Spring Festival on May 17th and 18th has the same procession.

At turns cosmopolitan and modern, others unerringly traditional, Japan can feel both familiar and otherworldly. Busy streets and language barriers can sometimes bamboozle visitors, but with a wonderfully efficient transportation system, well-developed tourism industry and advanced medical services and facilities, traveling in Japan is by and large safe and fairly straightforward. As a quick primer on the practicalities of traveling the country, the A–Z guide that follows will help you get the most out of your visit, with the minimum of fuss.

Arriving in Japan

The majority of inbound travelers arrive at Narita Airport, the main gateway to the country, which is 60 km (37 miles) east of Tokyo, in Chiba Prefecture. Despite a faster train connection having been added in 2010, you can still expect to take up to 90 minutes to reach terminal stations in central Tokyo after clearing customs. After that add another 30 minutes to find your bearings among the crowds and get a taxi, subway or train to your hotel. A good way to get into Tokyo is to take the JR Narita Express train, which runs once or twice hourly at a cost of ¥3,020 (when traveling from Tokyo to Narita but only ¥1,500 when traveling from Narita to Tokyo) and makes it to Tokyo Station in 56 minutes. An alternative is the Keisei Line, whose Skyliner service (2 or 3 hourly, ¥2,470) runs to Nippori in northeast Tokyo (next stopping at Ueno) in 36 minutes. Keisei's slower Access service (from ¥1,330) connects to Haneda Airport in southern Tokyo, on the way stopping at Asakusa (50 minutes) and Nihombashi (58 minutes).

Running more frequently are Airport Limousine bus services to Tokyo Station (every 15 to 30 minutes; ¥3,100; 80 minutes) and the Tokyo City Air Terminal (connected to Suitengumae subway station; every 10 to 15 minutes; ¥3,000; 55 minutes), although they can run into delays with traffic congestion. Taxi fares from Narita to within Tokyo start from ¥16,000 and can be as high as ¥26,500.

Besides Narita, many international flights now go to the more conveniently located Haneda Airport in Tokyo (30 minutes by train to central Tokyo), while the Kansai region is served by Kansai International Airport just outside Osaka. Trains, buses and airport limousines quickly transport travelers to Osaka, Kyoto and Kobe (kansai-airport.or.jp/en/access/bus/index.html/). Centrair Airport in Nagoya also hosts international flights (nagoya-airport-bldg.co.jp/en/access/).

Visas

Any visitor wishing to enter the country must be in possession of a passport that will remain valid for the full duration of their stay. Citizens of Australia, Canada, Ireland, New Zealand, the UK, the US and certain other countries can stay for up to 90 days if they are visiting for business or vacation. Citizens of Ireland and the UK can then extend their stay for an additional 90 days while in Japan. Citizens of other countries will need to leave Japan and then re-enter to do the same.

If you are a citizen of a country not mentioned above, you may need to arrange your visa in advance. For more information on this or for details of working and longer stay visas, you should contact your nearest Japanese consulate or embassy. Details are also available in English on the website of Japan's Ministry of Foreign Affairs: mofa.go.jp

Train and Bus Passes

Several pre-paid cards are now in use throughout Japan: SUICA, ICOCA and PASMO. Other regions now have similar pre-paid cards, but it is best to check if they function in all areas. The cards are valid on virtually all trains, subways and buses in Tokyo, Yokohama, Osaka, Kyoto, Nagoya and Fukuoka and several other areas with the following exceptions. As of 2017, the above three cards can be used on the Tokaido-Sanyo Shinkansen but not for some express trains, airport limousines and highway buses.

The card requires a ¥500 deposit when purchased. Thereafter you enter a desired amount of money for use on most trains and buses serving metropolitan areas except Kanazawa. The purchaser's name is not on the card so it is best to add small amounts when needed. There are fare adjustment machines whereby one can do this if the amount is insufficient when disembarking.

An invaluable site for finding transport route and fare calculator information is jorudan.co.jp/company/english/

There are a number of passes you can purchase for your intercity travels, the most popular being the JR Pass. This can only be purchased outside of Japan. You'll have to swap your exchange order for the JR pass at the JR station office when you arrive. jrpass.com

Calendar of Events

Japan has numerous annual national holidays. While banks, government offices, post offices and many companies close on these dates, most restaurants, shops and tourist attractions will remain open. The main holiday periods are O-bon (a week around August 15th), the New Year holiday (December 30th to January 3rd or 4th) and Golden Week (when multiple national holidays fall between April 29th and May 5th). Be aware that travel costs can spike during these periods, reservations can be harder to come by and popular sightseeing areas get crowded.

JAPAN'S NATIONAL HOLIDAYS

January 1st New Year's Day
Second Monday in January Coming of Age Day
February 11th National Foundation Day
March 20th or 21st Vernal Equinox
April 29th Greenery Day
May 3rd Constitution Memorial Day
May 4th National People's Day
May 5th Children's Day
Third Monday in July Marine Day
August 11 Mountain Day
September 23rd or 24th Autumn Equinox Day

Third Monday in September Respect for the Aged Day
Second Monday in October Sports Day
November 3rd Culture Day
November 23rd Labor/Thanksgiving Day
December 23rd Emperor's Birthday

There are many other annual and bi-annual celebrations and festivals that aren't designated as national holidays and a trip to Japan will no doubt coincide with some. For more information about these, visit the Japan National Tourism Organization's home page, jnto.or.jp, or see Festivals and Events on pages 111–14.

Climate and Seasons

Japan, as you'll frequently be reminded in tourist brochures, has four distinct seasons. You may be left wondering if some Japanese actually believe they are the only country to have four seasons. More perplexing is that besides spring (*haru*), summer (*natsu*), autumn (*aki*) and winter (*fuyu*), Japan arguably has a fifth season—rainy season (*tsuyu*)— before the onset of summer.

In winter, the temperature rarely drops below 0 °C and can often be in excess of 10 °C, except in the mountains, northern Honshu and Hokkaido. Like the sub-zero temperatures, heavy snowfall (although it does on occasions turn Tokyo or Kyoto white for a few days), is also generally restricted to northern Honshu, Hokkaido and mountainous areas. Otherwise central, western and eastern Japan are generally quite dry, mild and very often sunny, while winter in the south often feels more like a northern European springtime.

The first hints of spring come with the delicate buds of plum blossom in early to mid-March. This is soon followed by a pink front of cherry blossom that spreads northward across the archipelago in late March and early April, signaling the arrival of pleasant temperatures that will last through May. Separating spring from summer, everywhere except in Hokkaido, is a three- to four-week rainy season in June, during which the heat and humidity start to rise.

From July the rain gives way to clear summer skies, occasionally punctuated by a typhoon front that last through to late September. Summer high temperatures in all but the north and mountainous regions only infrequently fall below 30 °C and the midnight lows are typically around 25 °C. The mercury will often soar and stay in the mid- or even high 30s and be accompanied by oppressive humidity, so it's important to take precautions against heatstroke when out and about sightseeing. It's also a great time for scheduling a trip to the cooler mountains or the more temperate north.

After several months of sweating and lethargy, autumn is met with open arms when the temperatures begin to cool in October. Autumn is when Japan's natural beauty shines the most. The mountains and woods take on rich autumnal tones, the chrysanthemums bring parks and gardens to life, the skies stay clear, the air feels fresh again and the high temperature hovers in the low to mid-20s.

Electricity

The electrical current in eastern Japan, including Tokyo, is 100 volts, 50 hz alternating current (AC). In western Japan, including Kyoto, Nagoya and Osaka, it's 100 volts, 60 hz AC. Japanese sockets take plugs with two flat pins, so you may need to bring an adaptor. Nowadays domestic appliances can be used without adaptors throughout the archipelago.

Etiquette

As a foreign visitor, you'd have to do something spectacularly inappropriate to offend the Japanese. In fact, most cultural or social faux pas will probably be met with a smile; foreigners simply aren't expected to know any better. And although many a book has been written to bamboozle visitors in the finer points of Japanese etiquette, you don't need to worry about the intricacies of when, how and to whom to bow (a simple nod of the head will suffice to return a bow) or sweat on the correct way to hold your rice bowl. There are a few key points of etiquette, however, that you should make an effort to get right.

- If you have the opportunity to try a communal **bath** at a traditional inn (*ryokan*), public bathhouse (*sento*) or hot spring (*onsen*), don't get into the bath dirty or soapy. Use the separate wash area near the baths to shower and then rinse well before getting into the communal bathtub, making sure to get in naked and not let your wash cloth enter the water.

- You will always need to remove your outdoor **footwear** and change into slippers (which will be prepared for you) or socks whenever you enter a *ryokan* guestroom or someone's house. The same rule applies at many temples, shrines and even restaurants. The best way to judge when shoes aren't allowed is to look out for slippers at the entrance. If there are slippers lined up, use them, then leave your shoes by the entrance or, if available, store them in a foot locker. Once inside, remember to remove your slippers before stepping on any *tatami* mat flooring.

- Never stand **chopsticks** upright in a bowl of rice and never pass anything from chopstick to chopstick as both have associations with death and funerals.

- More important than focusing on what not to do, is to remember what you can do. Making the effort to say something as simple as *arigato* (thank you), *sumimasen* (excuse me) or *gochisosama deshita* (thank you; said after eating), will leave a lasting impact on the Japanese you meet.
- Regarding clothing, the kimono is the ultimate in non-revealing wear. When in doubt, remember that the Japanese prefer a wrapped package to an open gift (especially when visiting a temple).
- Tattoos are still not well received. Some bathhouses and swimming pools deny entry or ask that one cover the tattoo before entry. This is to relieve the anxiety of the other bathers and swimmers since tattoos are connected to crime. However, efforts are being made to accommodate visitors.

For a far more comprehensive guide to etiquette, visit the Japan National Tourism Organization's website: jnto.or.jp

For Disabled Travelers

Japan isn't the easiest country to get around for travelers with disabilities. Only a third of the country's train stations are fully accessible and many other public places lack basic facilities such as wheelchair ramps. Although major urban hotels tend to have wheelchair friendly rooms and accessible public areas, *ryokan* and smaller hotels are often lacking such facilities.

Trains have an area in at least one carriage designated for wheelchair users. Station staff can direct you to this and can also be called upon to help wheelchair users get on and off the train using a fold-up ramp they keep in the station office to negotiate the gap between the train and platform. Some stations also have chair lifts to get to and from the platforms.

On the plus side, most newer public buildings and department stores or malls will have barrier-free toilets, access ramps and wide elevators. Many taxi companies also now have cars with chair lifts, though these typically require booking at least an hour in advance.

For a list of accessible hotels and lots of other useful information, visit the Japan Accessible Tourism Center: japan-accessible.com/tips.html

Health and Safety

Japan is by and large a safe country. It has an advanced medical services infrastructure, and in most urban areas you will be able to find a major hospital or clinic that can treat you in English. Additionally, the drinking water is safe across the country and there are no major insect- or water-borne diseases. Japan also has no requirements for pre-travel inoculation against known diseases.

Over-the-counter **drugs and medications** are widely available at pharmacies, although in most cases the brands will be different to those from home and usage instructions will likely be in Japanese only. It's a good idea to bring a few basic medications with you as a precaution, such as painkillers, cold and flu medicine, stomach medicines and so on. If you are traveling with a pre-existing condition, you should also carry copies of any prescriptions and be sure to bring enough medicine for the duration of your stay. It's also a good idea to carry proof of medical insurance and a note of your blood type and any allergies you have.

If you need to visit a **doctor** during your trip, most large hotels have access to on-call medical services and others will be able to direct you to a nearby hospital or clinic. There are also several **emergency and non-emergency help lines** offering English-language services that can help locate medical care and provide interpretation where necessary (see Useful Telephone Numbers, page 124). All emergency service phone lines can handle English-language calls.

Japan has relatively low **crime** rates and incidents of personal robbery or violence are low, but it is still necessary to take basic precautions for personal safety. One potential issue faced by female travelers is groping on public transportation. If it happens, scream *chikan* to alert other passengers and contact the station staff when the train comes to a stop. Alternatively, look for the **women-only carriages** now available on most trains and subways during peak travel times.

One danger particular to Japan is **earthquakes**. The country experiences thousands of mostly unfelt tremors annually. While the chances of your visit coinciding with a big quake are slim, it's still worth becoming familiar with escape routes at your hotel and evacuation zones nearby, and spending a few minutes learning how to react to a tremor. **If a major earthquake hits, here's what you can do.** Stay away from windows as the glass can splinter, and if you can, draw the curtains or blinds. If you are inside, stay there, taking cover under something sturdy such as a table. If you have time before taking cover, open any nearby doors to prevent them from jamming and blocking your way out later. If you are outside, go to the nearest open space, such as a park, where you'll be safe from falling objects. In coastal areas, get to high ground as soon as the shaking subsides and stay there; more than 90% of deaths from the March 11th, 2011 earthquake were attributed to the subsequent tsunami. As soon as possible after the quake, contact your embassy.

Heat, too, can be dangerous. Be sure to keep hydrated in summer and take other precautions against **heatstroke**, which sends upward of 50,000 people to hospital every summer in Japan.

Internet

Most Western-style hotels offer free in-room Wi-Fi or broadband access, or failing that will have a terminal or computer in the lobby available free to guests. Those that don't provide free access will often offer a paid service for a daily fee of around ¥1,000. It's far less likely to find Internet access in a *ryokan* or *minshuku*, although some do have a shared terminal or computer available to guests.

Besides hotels, many international exchange centers run by local city and prefectural offices also offer free Internet access, and there are also many Internet cafés across the country where you can access a computer for a fee of around ¥200 to ¥400 per hour. Tourist offices will usually have a list of such places.

Money Matters

The currency of Japan is the yen. The universal symbol is ¥ but sometimes it will be written in the original Japanese, 円, pronounced *en*. Bank notes come in denominations of ¥1,000, ¥2,000 (not accepted by machines), ¥5,000 and ¥10,000. Coins come in ¥1, ¥5 (the only one without Western numerals, but recognizable because of the hole in its center), ¥10, ¥50 (also with a hole), ¥100 and ¥500.

Japan is still predominantly a cash society, but credit cards are becoming increasingly accepted. Amex, JCB, Visa and Master Card are widely accepted in hotels, restaurants, bars, taxis and shops in Tokyo and other large cities or popular tourist destinations, but it is always advisable to check beforehand. Outside of the bigger urban areas, make sure to carry ample cash just in case.

Traveler's checks in US, Canadian and Australian dollars, Sterling and Euros can be exchanged at larger banks and at main post offices. ATMs at most post offices will also accept foreign-issued cards, including those using Amex, Cirrus, Maestro, Master Card, Plus and Visa. Seven Bank ATM (found in 7-Eleven convenience stores and some Aeon and Jusco department stores) and Citibank ATM (citibank.co.jp) will also take overseas cards. As of July 2018, ¥108 is worth approximately US$1.

Tipping is not done in Japan. Trying to tip somebody might even cause embarrassment or offense. When you receive good service, simply saying thank you (*arigatou*) and smiling will more than suffice.

Opening Hours

Although many office workers remain in their offices well after 5 p.m., Japan in most other senses is a 9 to 5 country. **Post offices** tend to stick to a 9 a.m. to 5 p.m., Monday to Friday schedule for most services (though the ATMs often open longer), with main branches operating on shorter hours on weekends. **Banks** are only open on weekdays from 9 a.m. to 3 p.m., although bank ATMs usually remain open until at least 8 p.m., with those in convenience stores open 24/7 year round. **Department stores** and other bigger shops typically open daily from 10 a.m. to 7 or 8 p.m., while **smaller stores** and shops in local areas may stay open later. **Museums** typically close on Mondays (or the following day if Monday falls on a national holiday),

but remain open on weekends and national holidays, generally from 9 a.m. to 5 p.m. **Doctors' and dentists'** offices tend to open in the morning, then close for lunch before opening again in mid-afternoon, a typical schedule being 10 a.m. to 1 p.m. and 3.30 p.m. to 7 p.m. With all opening times, remember that banks, government offices, post offices, some tourist offices and many companies close on national holidays, during O-bon, and especially during the New Year holiday (see Calendar of Events, page 117).

Mobile Phones and Wi-Fi

If you own a smartphone, you should be able to use it in Japan. Just get a 4G data SIM card from the airport or electronic stores like BIC Camera and Yodobashi Camera. Otherwise, rent a pocket Wi-Fi router from your home country or online and have it delivered to your accommodation. Some Airbnbs will also provide you with one. Download applications like Japan Connected-free Wi-Fi, Free Wi-Fi Passport or Travel Japan Wi-Fi to access about 150,000 to 400,000 hotspots around the country for about two weeks after registration.

Dialing Codes

Japan country code: 81; Domestic area codes (to be omitted when dialing from within the same area): Hiroshima 082; Kobe 078; Kyoto 075; Matsuyama 089; Nagasaki 095; Nagoya 052; Naha 098; Nikko 0288; Osaka 06; Sapporo 011; Takamatsu 087; Tokyo 03; Yokohama 045

Useful Telephone Numbers
EMERGENCY AND HEALTH
Police emergency: 110
Police general inquiries: 03-3503-8414
Fire and ambulance: 119

Tokyo Metropolitan Health and Medical Information Center (for help finding English-speaking clinics and hospitals and arranging emergency interpretation): 03-5285-8181 (9 a.m. to 8 p.m. daily)

The AMDA International Medical Information Center (emergency and non-emergency medical assistance for non-Japanese speakers): 03-5285-8088 (Tokyo)/06-4395-0555 (Osaka)

Japan Help Line (Toll-free, 24-hour, multilingual emergency assistance service): 0120-461-997

Time

The whole of Japan operates in a single time zone, which is nine hours ahead of Greenwich Mean Time, 14 hours ahead of Eastern Standard Time and 17 hours ahead of Pacific Standard Time. Japan doesn't observe daylight saving time.

Traveling With Kids

If you are traveling with children young enough for **pushchairs**, it's a good idea to travel with a chair that is light and easy to fold away. As many stations don't have elevators or escalators, you could be carrying the pushchair often. Also bring a sufficient supply of **diapers**, **baby food** or any other such products, as although Japan has all the items you will need, you'll likely struggle to find familiar brands.

On **buses**, **trains** and **subways**, children under 6 get to travel free, while kids aged 6 to 11 travel half fare. Places such as **museums** and **amusement parks** usually offer discounted admission to children, which can be up to a 50% saving (see pages 103–5).

Restaurants often have low-price child meals available (ask for the *oko sama setto*; lit. children's set, or *kidozu menyuu*) and should be able to provide highchairs and children's cutlery.

Breastfeeding in public isn't a taboo but most women tend to avoid it or do so discreetly. Department stores always have private breastfeeding rooms and a place for changing diapers, as do some public buildings.

When booking a **hotel**, it's worth remembering that Western-style rooms that can accommodate more than three people are scarce. Some of the bigger (and more expensive) international chains will have large rooms available, but otherwise Japanese-style *ryokan* or *minshuku*, where you share a large *tatami* mat room that can accommodate lots of *futon*, are a great option.

Survival Japanese

With three different sets of characters (2,136 Chinese *kanji* characters for regular use as well as 48 *hiragana* and 48 *katakana* characters), Japanese at first glance appears to be a very difficult language to grasp. Learning to read and, in particular, write Japanese can indeed take many years. However, given the limited number of vowels and the fixed nature of their pronunciation, it isn't difficult to learn a few useful phrases for your holiday.

A BRIEF GUIDE TO PRONUNCIATION

Throughout this book when referring to place names or Japanese terms such as Tokyo or Shogun (correctly Toukyou and Shougun), the long vowel has been omitted. In the section that follows, however, long vowels are indicated to give the correct Japanese pronunciation.

Consonants are basically pronounced similarly to English, with the exception that g is always a hard sound (as in get). Vowel sounds work differently, as follows.

a as in **a**mong	e as in r**e**d
i as in ton**i**	o as in h**o**t

u as in p**u**t
ae is two sounds: a (as in c**a**t) and e (as in r**e**d)
ai as in Th**ai**land and ei as in sl**ei**gh
ie is two sounds: i (as in ton**i**) and eh
ue is two sounds: ooh and eh

BASIC PHRASES

Good morning *Ohayo gozaimasu*
Hello *Konnichiwa*
Good evening *Konbanwa*
Good night *Oyasumi nasai*
Goodbye *Sayonara*
My name is Smith *Smith (sumisu) to moshimasu* (polite)/*Smith (sumisu) desu* (informal)
It's nice to meet you *Hajimemashite*
Yes *Hai*
No *Iie*
OK *Ookei* (as in English)
Please *Onegai shimasu*
Please (offering something) *Douzo*
You're welcome *Dou itashimashite*
Thank you *Doumo* (casual)/*arigato* or *arigatou gozaimasu* (standard)/ *doumo arigatou gozaimasu* (formal)
I understand *Wakarimashita*
I don't understand *Wakarimasen*
Excuse me/pardon *Sumimasen*
Do you speak English? *Eigo wa dekimasu ka?*
How do you say it in Japanese? *Nihongo de nante iimasuka?*
What is this called? *Kore wa nan to iimasuka?*

AT THE HOTEL

I have a reservation *Yoyaku shite arimasu*
Do you have a room available? *Akibeya arimasu ka?*
How much is it per person/per room? *Hitori/heya wa ikura desu ka?*
Hotel *Hoteru*
Traditional Japanese inn *Ryokan*
Guesthouse/B&B *Minshuku*
Key *Kagi*

HEALTH

Hospital *Byouin*
Doctor *Isha*
Dentist *Haisha*
Pharmacy *Yakkyoku*
Medicine *Kusuri*
Fever *Netsu*
Diarrhea *Geri*
Pain *Itami*
Cough *Seki*
Nausea *Hakike ga suru*
I have a headache/stomachache *Atama/Onaka ga itai*
I'm ill *Byouki desu*
I have a cold *Kaze ga hikimashita*
I have the flu *Infuruenza desu*
Food poisoning *Shoko chuudoku*
I'm allergic to (nuts) *(nattsuu) arerugi desu*
Painkillers *Chin tsuyaku*
Stomach medicine *Igusuri*
Antiseptic *Shoudoku*
Antibiotics *Kosei busshitsu*

DIRECTIONS

(Excuse me,) where is the toilet? *(Sumimasen,) toire wa doko desu ka?*
(Excuse me,) is there a bank near here? *(Sumimasen,) chikaku ni ginkou wa arimasu ka?*
Straight ahead *Masugu*
On the left *Hidari ni*
On the right *Migi ni*
Police box *Kouban*
Bank *Ginkou*
Station *Eki*
Hospital *Byouin*
Pharmacy *Yakkyoku*
Department store *Depaato*
Supermarket *Supaa*
Convenience store *Conbini*

TRANSPORTATION

Train station *Eki*
Train *Densha*
Subway *Chikatetsu*

Bus *Basu*
Bus stop *Basu tei*
Airport *Kuukou*
Taxi *Takushii*
Bicycle *Jitensha*
Ferry *Ferii*
Ticket *Kippu*
Ticket office *Kippu uriba*
One-way *Katamichi*
Return *Oufuku*
Window/Aisle seat *Madogawa/tsurou-gawa no seki*
Non-smoking seat *Kinen seki*
I want to go to (Ginza) *(Ginza) e ikitai no desu ga.*
Reserved seat *Shitei seki*
Non-reserved seat *Jiyuu seki*

WINING AND DINING
Restaurant *Resutoran*
Bar *Nomiya*
Café *Kissaten/Kafe*
Pub-cum-restaurant *Izakaya*
Cafeteria *Shokudo*
Street food stall *Yatai*
Breakfast *Asa gohan*
Lunch *Hiru gohan*
Dinner *Ban gohan*
Menu *Menyuu*
Do you have an English menu? *Eigo no menyuu ga arimasu ka?*
I would like (some water) *(Mizu) o onegai shimasu*
Could I have the bill, please? *O-kaikei o onegai shimasu.*
Thank you for the meal (said to staff when leaving a restaurant or to people at your table when finishing your meal) *Gochisosama deshita*

SHOPPING
How much is (this)? *(kore) wa ikura desu ka?*
Do you accept credit cards? *Kurejitto kaado wa tsukaemasu ka?*
Cash *Genkin*

It's too expensive *Taka sugimasu*
I'll take this *Kore o kudasai*
Do you have...? *... wa arimasu ka?*

NUMBERS
Counting in Japanese can be challenging. Different systems are used for counting 1 through 10 for different things, and numbers are used in combination with a mind-boggling array of qualifiers. From 11 onwards, thankfully, there is basically a single set of numbers although the qualifiers remain equally confusing.

One to ten for objects

1 *Hitotsu*	6 *Muttsu*
2 *Futatsu*	7 *Nanatsu*
3 *Mittsu*	8 *Yattsu*
4 *Yottsu*	9 *Kokonotsu*
5 *Itsutsu*	10 *Tou*

Example: I'd like two beers, please: *Biiru o futastu kudasai.*

Common numbers for time, quantities and measurements

1 *Ichi*	6 *Rokku*
2 *Ni*	7 *Shichi* or *Nana*
3 *San*	8 *Hachi*
4 *Yon* or *Shi*	9 *Kyuu* or *Ku*
5 *Go*	10 *Juu*

11–19 *Juu-ichi, Juu-ni, Juu-san,* etc.
20 *Nijuu*
21–29 *Nijuu-ichi, Nijuu-ni, Nijuu-san,* etc.

30 *Sanjuu*	40 *Yonjuu*
50 *Gojuu*	100 *Hyaku*
1,000 *Sen*	10,000 *Ichi-man*
100,000 *Juu-man*	

MONEY
Bank *Ginkou*
Foreign exchange *Gaikoku kawase*
100 yen *hyaku en*; 1,000 yen *sen en*; 10,000 yen *ichi-man en*; 100,000 yen *juu-man en*

INDEX

PHOTO CREDITS

About Tuttle: "Books to Span the East and West"

Our core mission at Tuttle Publishing is to create books which bring people together one page at a time. Tuttle was founded in 1832 in the small New England town of Rutland, Vermont (USA). Our fundamental values remain as strong today as they were then—to publish best-in-class books informing the English-speaking world about the countries and peoples of Asia. The world has become a smaller place today and Asia's economic, cultural and political influence has expanded, yet the need for meaningful dialogue and information about this diverse region has never been greater. Since 1948, Tuttle has been a leader in publishing books on the cultures, arts, cuisines, languages and literatures of Asia. Our authors and photographers have won numerous awards and Tuttle has published thousands of books on subjects ranging from martial arts to paper crafts. We welcome you to explore the wealth of information available on Asia at **tuttlepublishing.com.**

Other books of interest from Tuttle Publishing
www.tuttlepublishing.com

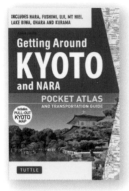

ISBN 978-4-8053-0964-3

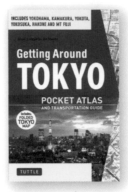

ISBN 978-4-8053-0965-0

ISBN 978-4-8053-1233-9

ISBN 978-4-8053-1137-0

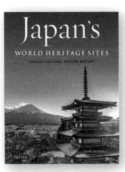

ISBN 978-4-8053-1475-3

ISBN 978-4-8053-1385-5

ISBN 978-4-8053-1441-8

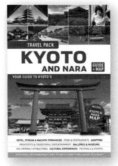

ISBN 978-4-8053-1179-0

ISBN 978-4-8053-1066-3